D0107305

Advance Praise

Without execution, there is no need for strategy.
We need to learn more about execution. Jeroen De Flander has added an-
other chapter to the emerging science of strategy execution.

PROFESSOR ROBERT KAPLAN,
HARVARD BUSINESS SCHOOL & DR DAVID NORTON

The Execution Shortcut *is a fantastic read! It is full of wonderful advice*
and practical examples and explains in a clear and engaging style how to
get your ideas or strategies implemented. You will not only enjoy reading this
book—you will act on it!

COSTAS MARKIDES,
PROFESSOR OF STRATEGY & ENTREPRENEURSHIP, LONDON BUSINESS SCHOOL

To create a better future, great ideas alone will not make the difference.
What we need are great decisions on the execution road. This book ex-
plains in an engaging way how Just Do It's don't come automatically. It
only happens when the mind is triggered, the heart inspired, and willpower
strengthened.

BERT STEVENS,
VICE PRESIDENT EUROPE OPERATIONS, NIKE

Jeroen De Flander has done it again!
In The Execution Shortcut, *an outstanding companion to his earlier work*
Strategy Execution Heroes, *he employs engaging stories, scientific rigor, and*
many compelling case studies that demonstrate the power of engaging the
head, heart and hands in your organization.

PAUL NIVEN,
BEST-SELLING AUTHOR *BALANCED SCORECARD, STEP-BY-STEP*

The Execution Shortcut *gives a refreshing insight into how*
to make your strategy a success on the work floor. I can recommend this book
to any leader, in particular in a multicultural environment where the con-
nection between head, heart, and hands is even more important to create
successful strategy execution.

PATRICK BODART,
PRINCIPAL DIRECTOR, EUROPEAN PATENT OFFICE

THE EXECUTION SHORTCUT

**Why Some Strategies Take
the Hidden Path to Success and Others
Never Reach the Finish Line**

Jeroen De Flander

the performance factory | *it's all about
strategy execution*

The Execution Shortcut
Why Some Strategies Take the Hidden Path to Success
and Others Never Reach the Finish Line

Published by *the performance factory*
Louizalaan 149/24 Avenue Louise, 1050 Brussels Belgium
www.the-performance-factory.com
Cover design: Jana Keppens

To report errors, please send a note to errata@the-performance-factory.com

Publications of *the performance factory* are available via amazon.com or amazon.co.uk. For bulk purchase, please contact bulk@the-performance-factory.com

ISBN 978-908148736-8
NUR: 801, 808 I BIC: KJC, KJMB I BISAC: BUS063000, BUS071000, BUS059000
Keywords: Strategy, Leadership, Skills

For
Karen, Lauren, and Jonas
my fellow life travelers

[handwritten inscription: Glad to meet you in Dubai, Kind Regards, love ... Roy 2019]

About the Author

Jeroen De Flander is a seasoned international strategy execution expert and highly regarded keynote speaker. He has shared the stage with gurus like Michael Porter, Costas Markides, Roger Martin, Robert Kaplan, and David Norton and helped more than 21,500 managers in 30 countries master the necessary execution skills. His first book *Strategy Execution Heroes* reached the Amazon bestseller list in 5 countries and was shortlisted for Management Book of the Year 2012 in the Netherlands.

Jeroen is co-founder of *the performance factory*—a leading research, training, and advisory firm focused solely on helping individuals and organizations increase performance through best-in-class strategy execution.

He has worked with several business schools including London Business School, IMD, Vlerick, Solvay, and TiasNimbas. For several years, he was the responsible manager worldwide of the Balanced Scorecard product line for Arthur D. Little, a leading strategy consulting firm.

He has advised 50+ companies including Atos Worldline, AXA, Bridgestone, Brussels Airport, CEMEX, Credit Suisse, GDFSUEZ, Honda, ING, Johnson & Johnson, Komatsu, and Sony on various strategy and strategy execution topics.

Contents

SHORTCUT RESOURCES

CHAPTER 1

The Epic Quest for the 3 H's

O ne windy day in October 1987, a few minutes before noon, a 51-year-old man with an idea took to the stage of a posh hotel in Manhattan, New York. He wore a gray pinstripe suit and a matching red power tie. He looked fit, solid, and confident. Just like your typical chief executive.

Then he started to speak.

"I want to talk to you about worker safety" he kicked off with. He then highlighted the company's statistics, telling the crowd that numerous workers were so badly injured that they were forced to stay off work for a while. "Our safety record is better than the general American workforce, especially considering that our employees work with metals that are 1,500 degrees and machines that can rip a man's arm off. But it's not good enough," he told the crowd, "I intend to go for zero injuries."

The audience—a group of prominent Wall Street investors and

stock analysts—was utterly confused. This wasn't what they'd ex-pected at all. They'd imagined big promises about future earnings, a bold vision or talk of some serious cost cutting. Anything but a safety lecture.

As soon as the presentation was over, they scuttled out of the room. One financial advisor raced to a payphone in the hotel lobby, called his 20 largest clients and said, "The board has put a hippy in charge and he's going to kill the company." He then urged each of them to get rid of all their stock immediately, before the news came out.

It turned out to be the worst piece of advice he ever gave.

When the Aluminum Company of America—better known as Al-coa—failed to perform, they hired Paul O'Neill as their new CEO, hop-ing he could turn the tide. He did. In the end, he stayed with the com-pany for 13 years. Under his watch, Alcoa's injury rate fell to one-twen-tieth the US average. The stock price had risen to 5 times the level of 1987. If that financial advisor had told his clients to buy a million stock instead, they would have earned more than 1 million in dividends and their stock would be worth 5 million.

Even today, O'Neill's legacy lives on. Alcoa remains one of the saf-est companies in the world. In 2010, not one single employee day was lost due to injury in 82 percent of Alcoa factories. In fact, on average, you're more likely to get injured at an accountancy office or software company than by handling molten aluminum at Alcoa.

So how did that happen? Alcoa doesn't specialize in selling safe-ty equipment. They're into aluminum. You wouldn't have expected O'Neill's crazy idea to get very far. But somehow it did. As a result, a sluggish aluminum company became one of the most successful companies in the industry. And it went from strength to strength, long after the individual who had sparked its journey had left the company.

■ ■ ■

Early on December 14 2004 at a large industry convention, a 57-year-old man with an idea took to the stage. He said, "Here's what I think we should do. I think we should save 100,000 lives. And I think we should do that by June 14 2006—18 months from today. 'Some' is not a number and 'soon' is not a time. Here's the number: 100,000. Here's the time: June 14 2006—9am."

The audience—a large group of healthcare leaders—was surprised. This wasn't what they'd expected at all. Of course there was a problem. At the time, everyone knew that the improvement potential was huge. "Between the healthcare we have and the care we could have lies not a gap, but a chasm," concluded the US Institute of Medicine in 2001 in their landmark report about healthcare in the next century. But it's one thing to know about an execution gap, and another to close it. The road to the finish line was filled with road blocks. And the healthcare leaders just didn't see how Donald Berwick, CEO of a small not-for-profit organization, could mobilize 3,000 hospitals—75 percent of all US hospital beds—to buy in to his crazy idea to save 100,000 lives in 18 months.

But they were proved wrong.

Exactly 18 months later, Berwick took to the stage again and said, "Hospitals enrolled in the 100,000 Lives Campaign have collectively prevented an estimated 122,300 avoidable deaths and, as importantly, have begun to institutionalize new standards of care that will continue to save lives and improve health outcomes into the future."

On July 7 2010, Berwick left his position as president and CEO of the Institute for Healthcare Improvements (IHI). But his legacy lives on. By December 2008, 4,050 hospitals had joined the program. Eight states enrolled 100 percent of their hospitals in the campaign. Other countries like Brazil, Canada, and Denmark also embraced the program. On top of that, there was a clear spillover effect to other domains like the 100,000 Homes Campaign—a national movement of communities working together to find permanent homes for 100,000 of the country's most vulnerable homeless individuals and families by July 2014.

What's Berwick's secret? How can one individual with no hierarchical power inspire and guide thousands of executives, physicians, and nurses in 3,000 hospitals enough to save over 120,000 lives in 18 months? And how does the idea keep going strong long after the individual who sparked its journey has left?

THE EXECUTION SHORTCUT is a travel story about successful strategies. It's a story about big ideas and the travelers they meet on their path to success.

Our ambition is really simple. We want to discover the execution routes that successful strategies take and use these learnings to put our own ideas on the right track to success. Peering over the travel logs of successful strategies provides us with unique insights; they show us the execution path, the road blocks, and the ingenuity their creators used to overcome them. Our newly gathered wisdom helps us, as strategists, to improve our own execution efforts.

O'Neill's safety idea and Berwick's dream to save 100,000 lives are textbook examples of successful idea journeys. And although their organizations might sound as if they don't have very much—a 60,000-strong company with operations in 30 countries listed on the New York Stock Exchange and a not-for-profit organization with 75 employees—both ideas followed a very similar travel pattern on their way to success.

First of all, both ideas found a way into the *hearts* of the people involved. It tapped into their emotional side and made them care. And so they decided to become a part of its journey. "Why not share my *other* idea?," thought one low-level employee when he heard that O'Neill was looking for ideas to improve safety. He suggested grouping the painting machines in order to switch the pigments faster so they'd respond more flexibly to customer demands. "It was like he gave us the winning lottery numbers," an executive said. Within a year, the aluminum siding profits had doubled. Once the Alcoa employees believed they were part of something important, they all started to pile in.

It wasn't that the healthcare professionals hadn't known that lives could be saved. Every person in the room had been aware of that. But just knowing wasn't enough. It wasn't until that memorable December day when Berwick launched his bold idea that they really started to care. Somehow he found a way into their hearts.

The second remarkable characteristic shared by both journeys is that both ideas found its way into *their heads*. Travelers on the execution road understood what had to be done to succeed. Berwick's team scripted 6 simple interventions with matching tips and tools each hospital could easily embrace. For example, when a patient is on a ventilator, their head should be elevated at a 45-degree angle to avoid suffocation. Doctors and nurses alike were encouraged to draw a line on the wall behind the bed of every patient on a ventilator and to tell everyone—family, other patients, and janitors—to notify someone immediately if the patient's head dropped below the line on the wall.

At Alcoa, O'Neill installed a simple feedback loop. If someone was injured, the manager in charge had to report directly to him within 24 hours with a plan to prevent such an injury reoccurring. O'Neill made it very clear how they could contribute to the success of the idea.

And success is permanent. People keep pushing the idea forwards, long after the idea creator has left the scene. Take Alcoa. It's now a safer place than it was when O'Neill left. And every week, new hospitals all over the world join the program. Somehow, the idea has found a way into the hands of the people. The idea stuck—the third shared characteristic of both journeys.

Over the course of this book, we'll discover that this triple connection—Head, Heart, Hands—lies at the core of each successful strategy journey. We'll also discover that successful strategists found an answer to 3 crucial questions: (1) How do I make others *care* about my idea—care enough so they are willing to figure out how they can contribute to success; (2) How do I make others *aware* of what the idea is all about—aware enough so they can make autonomous decisions that positively impact success; (3) How do I keep others going and *energize* them enough to keep them traveling the execution path even when I'm not around?

The name given to this successful triple connection—the connection between a big idea and the travelers it meets on its execution path—is the H^3-*connection*. It's our gateway to traveling the Execution Shortcut.

1.
Villains on the Execution Road

We all have great ideas. And we often need the help of others to let them shine. But getting people to support our brainchild is easier said than done. We know—and have probably experienced firsthand—that people don't always do what we like them to do. Sometimes they just don't seem to care about our idea and we wonder why they don't see the same benefits that we're seeing. Sometimes they seem to make all the wrong moves and we wonder, "How difficult can it be?" And sometimes they just seem too busy with other things and we think, "Why don't you push a little harder." Just like we do.

We all struggle to get our ideas across. And that's because successful H^3-connections are much harder to make than many of us realize. And failure doesn't come so much because of the quality of the idea, but because of age-old, programmed human behavior. It turns out that human nature kills big ideas. Why not join me in the lab for a few interesting experiments?

Imagine you're sitting with 15 other people in a small room. The host asks your neighbor to tap out the rhythm of a famous song like *Happy Birthday* on the table. You have to guess the tune. How much chance do you think you have of guessing the song correctly?

You've just taken part in an experiment designed by Elizabeth Newton from Stanford University. Over the course of the study, Newton repeated the process 120 times. Only 4 songs—2.5 percent—were guessed correctly. Not many, is it? But here's the interesting thing. Before the Listeners tried to guess the song title, she would ask the Tapper and the Listeners to predict their success rate. While the Listeners thought they would get 10 percent of the songs right, the Tappers thought the Listeners would guess a whopping 50 percent of their songs.

Isn't that amazing? The average Tapper got the message across 1 time in 40, but they thought they'd hit a homerun 1 out of 2. They overestimated their communication abilities by a factor of 20. So what happened? Does tapping make you a poor judge of your abilities? The simple answer is yes. The scientific name for this human phenomenon is the *Curse of Knowledge*. Here's how it works. When a Tapper—the idea creator—taps the song, the tune is playing along in his head. He's hearing the melody to *Happy Birthday* in his head while tapping the song. But the Listeners don't hear that music. The only information they get is a strange Morse code. It's very hard for a Tapper to judge the quality of his taps as he can't undo the tune playing in his head while tapping. The knowledge has 'cursed' him.

If we transport the Curse of Knowledge to the business world, it's not difficult to imagine that when an idea creator—a CEO, manager, policymaker or entrepreneur—finishes communicating and thinks, "I'm sure everybody gets my great idea after my extensive communication efforts", he's probably reached no more than 3 percent of his target population. *Houston, we have a problem.*

. . .

But there's more. Let's try a second experiment. This time, draw an imaginary 'E' on your forehead with your finger.

Researcher Adam Galinsky of Northwestern University and his colleagues divided participants into two groups. Those from the first were primed to feel powerful. How? They had to recall and write about an incident where they had power over others. The other group was asked to write about an incident in which someone else had power over them. Next, all participants were asked to draw the letter 'E' on their foreheads.

Now, there are two ways to draw an imaginary 'E' on your forehead. One way is as if you're reading it yourself, with the solid bar on your left and the openings on the right. The other way is to draw the 'E' as if another person is reading it, with the solid bar on your right and the openings on the left. The first choice produces a backward and illegible 'E' from the viewer's perspective. The second choice leads to an 'E' that's backwards to you.

The result? Surprisingly, the high-power participants from the first group were 3 times more likely to draw a self-oriented 'E'. Galinsky argues that power makes us blind. What does it mean? It means that the more power we have, the harder we find it to imagine the world from someone else's perspective. We draw the letter backwards because we are used to others adapting to our point of view. It also means that the effect of the Curse of Knowledge is likely to be reinforced when the person communicating is the boss. *Houston, we might have a big problem.*

. . .

Science teaches us that idea creators misjudge the quality of their communication due to the Curse of Knowledge. The effect is tripled when the idea creator is, or believes he is, in a position of power. But human nature doesn't only impact the behavior of the idea creator. It also impacts the behavior at the receiving end.

Sheena Iyengar from Columbia University and Mark Lepper from Stanford set up their lab in the form of a tasting booth on 2 different Saturday's at Draeger's supermarket, an upscale grocery store in California. One week, they had 24 jams to sample on the table, and the next week only 6. Customers could try as many samples as they liked and received a $1 discount coupon for a jam of their choosing.

The first results were as expected. Over the course of a 5-hour period, 60 percent of people who passed the display of 24 jams stopped, while only 40 percent did at the stand with 6 on display. So more choice means greater initial appeal. But the surprise came when they looked at the sales figures. Thirty percent of the people who stopped at the '6 jam' booth used the coupon and bought jam, but only 3 percent bought something at the '24 jam' booth. People initially exposed to a limited number of options are much more likely to purchase the product than those given a greater choice.

So what happened? Science calls this human phenomenon *Decision Paralysis*, another villain on the execution road. Again, it's not a deliberate action, but rather an expression of innate human behavior, this time at the receiving end. When someone wants us to do something (like buying jam), but presents us with too many options (24 flavors), we're paralyzed. We can't decide.

■ ■ ■

Through a series of lab tests, I wanted to show you that our instinctive behavior complicates H³-connections. They are much harder to realize then we might think. We think we have communicated our idea, but in reality we didn't. We think others will buy in to our idea if we give them lots of options, but in reality they don't. But what would happen if we were totally in charge? Would our idea run into trouble when we are the ideas inventor, as well as the executioner? By being the sole responsible, it would cancel out communication issues and we could choose the exact number of options we feel comfortable with. Let's find out.

For many of us, a new year is a new start. We have a long list of ideas and we're full of gusto to make them happen. And off we go. We join the gym, start a diet or commit to spending more time with the kids. I'm no different. Every January I make my list. And on January 1 2001, a great idea made it onto my New Year's resolutions. It was an idea that got me more enthusiastic than all of the others put together. I was going to write a book.

Eager to get going, I quickly came up with a framework with my Arthur D. Little colleague Torsten Schumacher. The first outline looked promising, but it took quite some effort to find the time to brainstorm. After a busy day, I couldn't muster up the energy to get writing. And it seems that I'm no different in failure to most people. A British study of over 3,000 people showed that 88 percent break their New Year's resolutions. A massive 4 out of 5 don't follow through on their own great ideas. And they drop the ball after a few weeks.

The human phenomenon that makes us kill our own great ideas is called *Willpower Depletion*. It's the third villain on the execution road. Many scientific studies document this rather strange human behavior. Baumeister's 'cookie' experiment is one of the best known. Let's visit the lab one last time before we hit the road.

In the first part of the experiment, Baumeister's team kept 67 hungry participants in a room that smelled of freshly baked chocolate cookies. He teased them further by showing them the treats. Half of the group was allowed to dig in and eat the cookies and the second group was asked to eat radishes.

Next, Baumeister's team gave the participants a second, supposedly unrelated challenge. They had to trace a geometric figure without retracing any lines or lifting their pencils off the paper. After a brief test period, they were told that they had as many attempts as they wanted. They would be judged only on whether or not they could finish tracing the figure. If they wished to stop beforehand, they had to ring a bell.

Unknown to the participants, these geometric figures were impossible to solve. The researchers wanted to test the effect of Willpower Depletion. In other words, would the group who had eaten the cookies put in more execution effort than the group who had selected to eat radishes? The effect of the manipulation was immediate and undeniable.

On average, the cookie contestants kept going for 18 minutes, making 34 attempts to solve the puzzle. However, the radish group gave up after 8 minutes, having made only 19 attempts. As they had to resist the cookies and force themselves to eat vegetables, they could no longer muster the will to fully engage in another torturous task. They were already mentally exhausted. They ran out of willpower. The villain won.

■ ■ ■

When our new idea—whether it's a book project, a corporate strategy, a business plan for a new product launch or a policy to improve the education system—comes into contact with million-year-old human dynamics like Decision Paralysis, Willpower Depletion or the Curse of Knowledge, our idea is in trouble. These human complexities are so powerful that they can override our own rational thinking and stop us from executing our own ideas, as happens every New Year for 88 percent of the population.

These human dynamics—the execution villains—are the reason why most strategies take the long route to the finish line. If we aspire to get a better return from our strategy, then we must learn how these human behaviors impact the idea journey and how to deal with them.

The execution villains we'll meet offer us a way of making sense of the complex human dynamics that every strategy has to navigate. They provide us with direction on how to get our strategy into the heads, hearts, and hands of others. Thinking about the specific behaviors of the villains triggers fundamental *why* questions on the impact of human behavior on strategy. Why doesn't repeating the strategy message help create understanding? Why is business growth a slow strategy killer? And why do leaders tend to go overboard with the amount of measures? Thinking about tactics to outwit the bad guys on the execution road helps us answer important questions on *how* to make a successful H^3-connection. How do we trigger the right emotions with our strategy story? How do we pick and introduce habits that facilitate the decision process? And how can we increase commitment to the strategy?

2.
The Shortcut Roadmap

We learn from successful idea journeys such as the 100,000 Lives Campaign and Alcoa's zero injuries ambition that it all starts with a triple connection: our strategy needs to connect with the heads, hearts, and hands of those involved—the travelers. But we also learn from science that those connections are much more difficult to make than we think because of the intricacy of human nature.

This book offers a coherent set of tested moves—*a shortcut map*—to navigate these human complexities and make successful H^3-connections.

The elements on the map come from 30 years' behavioral and strategy research, hundreds of scientific studies from well-known universities including Harvard, Columbia, and Stanford, and an ambitious 12-year execution research project that tapped into the minds of 23,500 leaders in 29 industries and 36 countries. I started the project in 2001 with the research team from *the performance factory*, after leaving strategy advisory firm Arthur D. Little.

So it's fair to say I didn't invent the map. I'm just the cartographer, working together with a fantastic research team to pull all these pieces of wisdom together. But I'm a cartographer with a mission, an execution ambassador wanting to show you the benefits of sound execution. I'm convinced that's where most of us can make the difference.

To be honest, I'd traveled a long way before I became a believer myself. As a strategist, I was convinced a great strategy would produce great results. But reality didn't match up to my belief. The more I saw great strategies fail (some of which I helped develop), the more I knew the success formula was missing something.

Let's be clear. This doesn't mean that I lost my convictions about strategy. Former colleagues even joked that I'd turned over to the dark side, that I switched camps after I left Arthur D. Little. On the contrary, a good strategy is the starting point. Without a strategy, there's no race.

But what gets us to the starting line won't get us to the finish line. The long, winding execution road requires the attention of the leader. To succeed, a great leader needs to be a strategist as well as an execution hero. This message and the practical "how to" is detailed in my first book *Strategy Execution Heroes*.

But leaders don't make the execution journey alone. This book zooms in on the initial transfer, the connection between the strategists' big idea, and the others that will join them on the execution journey.

It's good to know that the shortcut is available to us all. We can all make others more aware of our big idea, make them care, and boost their energy levels to move it forwards. But the shortcut journey isn't a free ride. Traveling the execution shortcut requires effort. Don't expect to cruise a 5-lane highway in a red convertible on a Wednesday afternoon, wind blowing in your hair, stopping for a nice coffee. Instead, you should expect a long trek, carrying your own supplies, in a far-off country. The signposts are unreadable and you're with a group of fellow travelers who aren't sure if they should be following you or not. But what might initially feel like an impossible journey is just a tough hike across a country you don't know so well. You might even come to enjoy the trip.

In the end, to succeed as a strategist, we need a thorough understanding of what makes people tick. And that's on top of industry dynamics, customer behaviors, and financial savyiness. We need to have a deep understanding of how people process information and make decisions, what makes them care about an idea, and what gives them the energy to take action. And when we do, the execution shortcut becomes visible.

IN SEARCH OF the execution shortcut, we're going to venture out of the lab and into the real world. We'll go to Canada and find out about a crucial decision pattern. We'll go to Egypt and learn about the importance of 'no' in strategy. We'll go to a monastery high up in the Indian Himalaya to understand the importance of focus. And we'll meet amazing people like Stephen Denning who reshaped the future of the World Bank with a single strategy story. We'll also meet Ratan Tata who inspired 600 engineers to design the cheapest car in the world and Billy Beane who turned a crumbling baseball team into a winning machine. We'll join a South Pole expedition to learn about the power of habit, run a marathon to test the impact of measurement, and take a combat course to experience what happens if you truly believe in your abilities.

The point of all of this is to answer 2 simple questions that lie at the heart of what we would all like to accomplish as executives, managers, policymakers, and entrepreneurs. Why is it that some great strategies get executed and others don't? And what can we do to deliberately speed up and control successful strategy journeys of our own?

PART 1

HEAD

CHAPTER 2

Facilitate SMALL Choices

4 am Friday morning in a suburb of a large city. Lisa got out of bed. She always did at this early hour. The routine came with the job. Lisa worked as a mail carrier for the national mail company. On an average day, she made hundreds of mail drops to the city's apartment blocks and businesses. Lisa loved her job. And she was proud to be working in this industry with its long history. But more and more people used email and other communication channels to connect. She knew that the business—and therefore her job—was in danger.

While Lisa grabbed breakfast, her thoughts wandered to last week's meeting. One of the executives had come over to the sorting center to talk about the future of the organization. Lisa understood that her company was doing ok, but that it would need to do better to secure its future. More specifically, she understood that efficiency had to improve from 6 to 5 seconds per mail item and customer satisfaction from 75 to 80 percent. "I can do that", she had thought to herself after the meeting.

That Friday, on her 46th drop, an old lady opened her front door and waved Lisa over to talk. "Greater client satisfaction," thought Lisa, "but my delivery speed will reduce if I stop." She was paralyzed. "What should I do?" The choice seemed insignificant in comparison to all the other things this big organization needed to do to succeed. But it was her responsibility. And she wanted to do the right thing.

Now, think for a moment. What advice would you give Lisa? She saw 5 options: (1) To focus on efficiency, hurry to the next mailbox and pretend she didn't see the woman; (2) To focus on efficiency, but to acknowledge the old lady with a wave while walking to the next mailbox; (3) To focus on efficiency, but spend a few minutes on small talk; (4) To focus on quality and take all the time that's needed; (5) To focus on quality and try to sell the old lady something.

■ ■ ■

You've probably realized that the right answer isn't so straight-forward. When you focus on quality, you lose out on efficiency… and when you focus on efficiency, you lose out on quality. In short, the strategy message delivered by the executive makes Lisa's decision pretty difficult. Not difficult because of the efficiency-quality trade-off—trade-offs you'll find in every good strategy—but because of the missing prioritization information. Many employees face the same challenge as Lisa on a daily basis. How do I balance 2 contradictory strategy elements and still make the right decision?

1.
Strategy, A Choice Pattern

Professor Henry Mintzberg is an internationally renowned academic. He has written more than 150 articles and 15 books on business and management. One of Mintzberg's insights, "Strategy is a pattern in a stream of decisions," helps us to better understand how decisions relate to strategy. A long time ago, I learned this phrase by heart—but it took me 5 years to really grasp the point of it. The trick I use to understand Mintzberg's cryptic statement is to approach decisions in 2 steps. First, there's the overall decision—the *big choice*—that guides all other decisions. To make a big choice, we need to decide *who we* focus on—our target client segment—and we need to decide *how* we offer unique value to the customers in our chosen segment. That's basic strategy stuff. But by formulating it this way, it helps us to better understand the second part, the day-to-day decisions—the *small choices*—that get us closer to the finish line. When these small choices are in line with the big choice, you get a *Mintzberg Pattern*.

The Mintzberg Pattern is crucial to understanding successful strategy journeys. When we think and talk about strategy journeys, we think and talk about people and the decisions they make. Successful strategy journeys follow a Mintzberg Pattern, small choices that are in line with a big choice, like wagons that follow the train engine to its destination.

At first sight, from a strategist's point of view, the big decision seems like the tough one. But that's not quite right. Yes, defining a strategy is hard, but the power of small decisions—the day-to-day choices of all employees on the execution road—cannot be underestimated. If Lisa makes the wrong decision, the overall impact on the company is very limited *(and surely less impactful than making the wrong strategy choice)*. But if 10,000 colleagues make wrong judgments about quality and cost on a daily basis, then these small decisions aren't so small anymore. Think about Alcoa and its relentless focus on safety. If one person doesn't wear a helmet *(a small choice)*, the impact on safety is limited. It's unlikely that something would happen to *that* person on *that* day. But if everyone at Alcoa decides to wear helmets only occasionally, the accident risk increases exponentially. Small decisions do have a big impact on the success rate of strategy journeys, not because of their individual size or importance, but because of their *sheer number and exponential force*.

Most of us don't pay attention to these small decisions. And that's mainly because we find it difficult to grasp the logarithmic effect of wrong small choices. *(How much worse can it be if a few more people don't wear a helmet?)*.

Consider the challenge given to high school student Britney Gallivan of Pomona, California. If you fold a piece of paper in half 50 times, how thick would the end result be? Most of us would imagine the end result to look like a stack as big as a large phone book. We visualize 50 pieces of paper lying on top of each other. But the answer might surprise you. Gallivan decided to test it. She knew she needed a big piece of paper. After some searching, she found a 0.75-mile roll of toilet paper. With her parents, she rolled out the jumbo paper, marked the halfway point, and folded it once. It took a while because it was a long way to the end of the paper. Then she folded the paper a second time, then again and again. After 7 hours, she folded her paper for the 11th time into a skinny slab of around 31.5 inches wide and 15.75 inches high and posed for photos. In the end, she was able to fold the paper 12 times. If she could have folded it 17 times, the final stack would be taller than your average house. Three more folds and that sheet of paper would be a quarter of the way up the Burj Khalifa, the largest tower in the world. Ten more folds and it would have crossed the outer limits of the atmosphere. Another 20 and it would be about 60 million miles high, about two-thirds the distance to the Sun.

"The world was a great place when I made the twelfth fold," Gallivan wrote when documenting her experiment. She also explained the phenomenal exponential force of repetitive small actions, known as a 'geometrical expansion'. This is an important lesson for us. Taking into account the sheer number and exponential force, small decisions become SMALL. And successful strategists have SMALL decisions on their radar.

■ ■ ■

If strategy is a decision pattern, strategy execution is enabling people to create a decision pattern. In other words, strategy execution is helping people make *small* choices in line with a *big* choice. This notion requires a big shift in the way we think about execution. As a strategist looking at strategy execution, we should imagine a decision tree rather than an action plan. Decisions patterns are at the core of successful strategy journeys, not to-do lists. To improve execution speed and accuracy, we should shift our energy from asking people to make action plans to helping them make better decisions.

2.
Michael Porter's Surprising NO

Egypt, 2010, just before the Arab Spring. There were about 600 people—a mixed crowd of executives, entrepreneurs, professors, charity executives, and policymakers—in the Ballroom of the Grand Hyatt Hotel in Cairo. It was unseasonably hot for October. The delegates were excited, chattering loudly. Then Chairman Adham Abdel-Salam introduced the first speaker of the day. Harvard Professor Michael Porter took the stage at the Next Generation Strategy Conference. He talked animatedly about strategy, citing cases from IKEA and Paccar. He also explained the economics of strategy and talked about shared value, the next big thing in strategy. But my favorite part was still to come. Watching intently from my front row position, I wondered when he would talk about the importance of 'no'.

One of the most valuable lessons I learned from my discussions with Michael Porter is the importance of 'no' in strategy. "The essence of strategy is choosing what *not* to do," he likes to say. Let's take a closer look. At the start of each strategy journey, companies decide on their client offer. Over time, they tend to add new product features and services to their initial portfolio, trying to broaden their customer base and tap into new profit pools. This scope creep is hard to resist. We all know the arguments—our shareholders demand top-line growth, our customers want it, the marginal cost for adding a product feature is minimal, our competitors are doing the same.

But the scope creep, while understandable, is dangerous. By *diluting the underlying strategy trade-offs*, by adding water to wine, we lose our initial choice—our strategy. The dilution can happen on *the why side* of the choice. "While our focus is on small companies, this large company is so interesting. Let's service it too and see how it goes," is an example of a typical reflection. And on *the how side*, it often sounds like, "Let's offer a bit more service than we planned, just like our major competitor." But, by trying to be all things to all people, companies dilute their strategy. And very quickly, there's no strategy left.

At the end of a strategy exercise, the strategist has selected a core client segment and identified the distinct activities to offer unique value *(the 'yes')*. Inherent in this choice is a whole list of things that the company isn't going to do—customers that don't fit the chosen segment, activities that the company won't do *(the 'no')*. Successful strategists capture these noes and make them very explicit. Their instrument? *The List of Noes*. Each strategy should arrive at the start of the execution journey with a clear List of Noes. This list provides an answer to questions like: Which clients are we going to make unhappy? Which service aren't we going to deliver? Which product features aren't we going to add? What internal expenditure aren't we going to make?

A List of Noes is an essential element of a company's strategy journey. It's something to promote, to put in the sales window, not something to apologize for and hide away. "I'm as proud of what we don't do as I am of what we do," Steve Jobs said. If you find promoting the noes difficult, think about the following: some like water, some like wine, few like drinking a mix of both. We can't be all things to all people. If we try, we end up nowhere on our journey. Successful strategists make a choice—who and how—and decide to stick with that choice. They fight against choice dilution. Successful strategists proudly make and defend a List of Noes.

A clear 'no' at the strategy level also reduces the option list for small choices *(and therefore improves decision making)*. Let's take an easy example. Remember the jam experiment? We learned that a choice of 24 is too much. It paralyses the buyer. When you end up at the 24-jam booth and I want you to buy something, I need to reduce the number of options. To facilitate your shopping experience, I could point out that you shouldn't buy jam made from red fruits like strawberries, cherries or raspberries. (*No = we never buy red jam*). I could also add that you shouldn't buy either the most expensive or the cheapest. (*No = we never buy the cheapest or most expensive product or service*). I won't be able to eliminate all your options, but the 2 noes will probably have brought back the number into a range that circumvents Decision Paralysis. And that's one of the villains we want to outwit.

Let's see if we can reduce Lisa's options. To do so, we need to find a few noes at strategy level. Imagine we have a chat with her CEO. She tells us, "In order to get our company to the next level, we need to boost our customer orientation. We cannot accept employee behavior that goes against our clients. We exist because of our clients and should treat them that way. *(No = we never forget the customer comes first)*. It doesn't mean we all have to sell. Our mail delivery people, for example, shouldn't. It would make our supply chain too complex. *(No = we don't make our supply chain complex)*. But they do have to be customer oriented. That's what service is all about. And a smile doesn't cost money or time or complex processes. It's an attitude." If we translate this to Lisa's context, we could say to her that "Clients should never be ignored" and "Sales isn't part of your job." Knowing this, Lisa can strike out her first and last option. Only 3 left.

■ ■ ■

Mintzberg teaches us that decisions are at the heart of successful strategy journeys. Porter teaches us that a clear 'no' helps us to facilitate decision making. The List of Noes improves day-to-day choices by reducing the number of options. It helps us to combat the villain Decision Paralysis on the execution road. But there are still choices to be made. While the List of Noes is crucial to sharpen the big choice and eliminate *some* options, it doesn't eliminate *all* the options. We know that we don't want strawberry jam, but that leaves us with a bunch of other jams to choose from. We can tell Lisa that options 1 and 5 are clearly out-of-scope, but that still leaves her with 3 options to choose from. Our next challenge: how can we help others make the right choice from the remaining options?

3.
Decision First Aid

"No plan survives enemy contact" is a well-known army motto. You can define a brilliant set of moves against your opponent, but if that enemy decides to attack in a different way, your plan becomes useless. To overcome this problem, the army invented the 'Commander's Intent'—a set of specific instructions that captures the core of the combat strategy. It guides soldiers on the battlefield when they are forced to improvise against an unforeseen enemy move. The Commander's Intent provides soldiers with the core message, enabling them to make autonomous execution decisions in line with the overall purpose of the mission.

"No strategy survives contact with day-to-day reality" should be our motto. Just like generals can't foresee enemy moves on the battlefield, strategists can't foresee hazards on the execution road. And just like the army helps soldiers to independently make the right decisions to combat the enemy with the Commander's Intent, strategists have to do the same with travelers who face unforeseen execution challenges. When travelers face multiple options that can't be eliminated by the company's List of Noes, it's important that we help them. We can't expect the company owner, policymaker, CEO or manager to make all decisions using a decision hotline (although I know a few who would be tempted to try). That's not realistic. It's our job—just like the army generals—to enable people to make good execution decisions on their own.

Let's go back to the 24-jam booth. I gave you 2 clear noes. *(No red jam and not the most expensive or cheapest one)*. Let's see if I can further facilitate your decision process, not knowing what you'll find at the store. I could facilitate your shopping experience with the following information: "If in doubt, pick the jam with the lowest sugar percentage" and, "If there are still too many options left, pick the one the salesperson indicates as the most popular."

What I just did was give you prioritization information. These decision guidelines can't be too vague. Vague information on a journey sounds like "Travel safely" (*Pick the jam that tastes good),* or "Go north" *(Pick the jam that's not too expensive).* But when you unexpectedly come across a wild river on your route north, what do you do? *(The jam that tastes best happens to be quite expensive...).* Do you keep heading north, cross it anyway, and risk being swept away? Or do you travel safely and take a diversion, but risk losing valuable time? Being specific is a very important lesson. Often, our decision advice is vague and sounds like "Be client-oriented," or "Focus on costs." We put them forwards as decision aid, but they fail as they don't help rank the options on the execution road. Successful strategists provide travelers with specific prioritization information, not a general compass. This helps travelers make autonomous decisions in line with the strategy.

■ ■ ■

When regional concessions of the Rede Ferroviária Federal—the Brazilian state-owned railway system—were auctioned in the 90's, a private equity firm called GP Investimentos Limited bidded for the Southern line which served Parana, Santa Catarina, and Rio Grande do Sul. It won and paid 217 million Brazil real (approximately US$195 million at the time) for the renewable 30-year concession. Alexandre Behring, only in his early 30's at the time, became CEO.

Behring's road to success was daunting. While Brazil's economy was booming with an annual GDP growth of 8 percent, the railway branch he managed was in an appalling state. They were losing 80 million Brazilian reals a year, their cashflow was negative outside of the harvest season, and they needed hundreds of millions in investment to maintain and upgrade the physical assets required (an audit revealed that 50 percent of the bridges needed repair, with 20 percent close to collapse). But they had only 30 million in cash on the balance sheet. On top of that, the Southern line had an extremely poor accident record and technology was lagging a few decades behind.

But luckily, there were a few bright spots as well. After thorough analysis, Behring found there was a dormant demand for railway freight transport. At the time, the railway's market share compared to trucking was very low. Opportunities existed. To succeed, they had to find a way to take away business from the trucking companies. Behring also knew that a well-managed railway is a natural monopoly with clear cost advantages over trucking. *(They could compete on cost)*. But they were a long way off. To succeed, they had to restructure the company's cost base and boost management capabilities.

With limited funds in the bank, Behring didn't have much room to maneuver. Execution had to be flawless. To help employees make the right decisions in the field, Behring and his CFO Duilo Calciolari came up with 5 clear prioritization rules:

Rule 1. *Focus first on increasing revenue with existing clients.* They believed they could double sales with these customers in 3 to 4 years *(and it would be easier than finding new clients)*.

Rule 2. *Focus first on the most promising existing clients.* To help answer the question in the salesperson's mind, "Should I try to sell to this client first?," they developed a ranking system. They estimated a customer's potential benefit when transporting all goods via rail compared to trucking. Those with the highest potential ended up on top.

Rule 3.   *The best choice is the option that requires the least cash upfront*—even if the choice was more expensive in the long run or wasn't the most elegant solution.

Rule 4.   *The best choice is the option that solves the problem fastest*—even if the other solutions proved to be better in the long-term.

Rule 5.   *The best choice is the option that re-uses existing resources*—compared to buying new.

These hands-on prioritization rules helped employees to make the right on-the-job decisions. For example, when competitors were negotiating for new locomotives to fulfill increasing demand, their engineers were working 24/7 repairing old ones *(Rule 3: the least cash upfront; Rule 4: solves problem faster)*.

Their engineers also found a creative solution to the problem of damaged tracks. Rather than purchasing new rails costing US$400 per ton, they collected those from closed routes and installed them on active ones *(Rule 5: re-use existing resources)*.

Their strategy and execution focus paid off. The end result was impressive. They turned a net loss of 80 million into a net profit of 24 million in 2000. In 2003, after 6 years of hard work and strict prioritization, they doubled capacity from 11 million tons to 22 million, increased car utilization by 67 percent, and reduced diesel fuel consumption by 40 percent. And the company was named one of the 100 best places to work in Brazil.

There are many forks in the road on the execution path. It's easy for travelers to get lost. Behring offered his employees clear prioritization information to align their small choices with the big choice. By offering decision aid, he was able to create a Mintzberg Pattern. Behring guided his travelers to the finish line.

. . .

Remember Berwick and O'Neill? Both offered clear prioritization advice as well. At Alcoa, safety always comes first. If you have to choose between 2 options at Alcoa, the one with the most positive impact on safety wins. If you work for one of the hospitals enrolled in the 100,000 Lives Campaign, you have a clear script with 6 things to focus on. You have a clear decision pointer to help you make the right decisions to save lives.

Let's see if we can further facilitate Lisa's decision process. Imagine we talk to the mail carrier's CEO again. She says, "In order to survive in our industry, we need to tap into new profit pools. This demands a new client attitude. But if we don't keep our costs under control, we won't be in the game at all. So we need even more efficiency."

Reading between the lines, it's safe to say that efficiency comes first. Without efficiency gains, there's no money left to invest. From here, it's a small step to formulate prioritization information for Lisa. We could say, "When in doubt, focus on efficiency first." But let's be more ambitious. Let's try to put the decision aid into a context Lisa knows best... her job. To do so, we should take a closer look at what efficiency means for a mail carrier. We learn that each carrier has a specific time to make each drop, 5 seconds in Lisa's case. And a clear daily deadline—to finish the mail round without overtime. Knowing this, we could formulate the prioritization information as, "When in doubt, make sure you finish your daily round on time." *(Efficiency first in the context of Lisa's job).* If Lisa can increase client satisfaction within these limits, even better. So why not say, "Be friendly to your customers—smile, say hello, have a chat—but keep an eye on your watch. Always make sure you finish your round on time." *(Be friendly, engage with your customers, but don't have a coffee with every person you run into. Your customers might love you, but our company will go bankrupt).*

Like army generals, successful strategists provide travelers with prioritization information—*a Decision Intent*—in a context that fits their jobs. We point out the right decisions, without knowing exactly what forks in the road travelers will encounter on their journey.

■ ■ ■

We know now that daily choices, as in Lisa's mailbox dilemma, are an expression of the company's strategy—the big choice. We also know that successful strategy journeys can be recognized by their decision pattern—small choices in line with the big choice. The first might look like nothing compared to the second—not worthy of a strategist's time—but if we think about Britney Gallivan's paper-folding challenge, it puts small decisions in a different light. To take the execution short-cut, we have to enable travelers to make day-to-day decisions that fit the Mintzberg Pattern. So far, we've encountered 2 tactics to facilitate SMALL choices: (1) limit the options with a List of Noes and, (2) provide prioritization guidelines—a Decision Intent—for the remaining options. To learn the third tactic, let's take a trip to a hotel bar in Chile.

CHAPTER 3

Keep the Big Choice Clearly Visible

"If you get 150 people behind your idea, you've reached the tipping point. Then the idea will spread like a virus," a senior executive told me while we were having a drink at a hotel bar in Santiago, Chile. "You should really look into it. It's a great concept."

Jan was the fifth person to have told me enthusiastically about the tipping point. The other 4—an Indian MBA student living in the UK, a German VP who sat next to me on a plane, a Finnish CEO who loves to read business books, and a journalist from a respected magazine—all said the same thing: "Get 150 behind your idea and it will spread like a virus."

Pretty cool idea, right? You get 150 people to buy into your idea and then it snowballs to the finish line. Simple. Interested, I asked my discussion partner if he'd ever experienced this viral idea firsthand. "No," he replied, "A colleague advised me to give it a try. Apparently the concept comes from a book written by a Canadian named Malcolm

Gladwell. But I'm going to give it a try when I launch my next project. And you should too."

When we left the bar, I told him he was the fifth person to have given me the same advice. I joked that maybe there was some kind of conspiracy between them to give me this crucial message. He laughed, reassuring me that he'd never met the other 4 in his life.

During my flight back, I kept re-running the conversation in my head. More than anything, I was surprised. I'd read Gladwell's bestseller *The Tipping Point* a few years earlier, but I couldn't remember this 150 idea. I did remember the 'Mavens' and, most of all, the importance of message stickiness, a topic I became very fond off. But the 150 didn't ring a bell. I decided to re-read the book. I wanted to find out more about the idea that these 5 people had raved about, while I'd completely forgotten it.

Back home, a few days later, I finished the book for the second time. And I was even more confused. On the back cover, Gladwell defines 'a tipping point' as "That magic moment when an idea, trend, or social behaviour crosses a threshold, tips and spreads like wildfire." Gladwell does talk about the Rule of 150, but the message isn't directly linked to the book title. Specifically Gladwell says: "The Rule of 150 suggests that the size of a group is another one of those subtle contextual factors that can make a big difference." He refers to several studies that point out that groups that become larger than 150 lose their social glue. The core message: keep your group size *below* 150.

So how can 5 smart people living on 3 different continents end up talking about the same incorrect message? A message they care about so much that they pass it on to others? And why didn't they talk about the 2 things I did remember—the Mavens and the stickiness?

These 3 questions nagged away at me for weeks. I tried to come up with a solution. Maybe they did know each other after all and had discussed it together? No, I reminded myself, this isn't a James Bond movie, this is real life. Maybe they'd all heard a talk by the same person who had also misunderstood the idea? Unlikely. Most people don't travel across continents to listen to speeches and that would be some coincidence. So maybe I just didn't get the point of the book? Could be. So I read the book again, paying special attention to the 150. But by now, I was convinced that the 2 key elements of the message—the Rule of 150 and the tipping point—were not related to each other as those 5 people had described. The Rule of 150 is a limiting factor, rather than an accelerator. If we want groups to serve as incubators for an idea, we have to keep the group size below 150. To validate that, I scoured the web and thankfully discovered that most websites offered an explanation in line with my own understanding. I wasn't going crazy. But, funnily enough, around one in 20 connected the tipping point with the Rule of 150, as did the 5 people I'd spoken to. Despite my efforts, I couldn't solve the mystery. That is, until Sherlock Holmes crossed my path…

1.
The Tripping Point

Sir Arthur Conan-Doyle wrote his first Sherlock Holmes story in 1886. The fictitious character was based on a real man, Dr Joseph Bell, a renowned forensic scientist at Edinburgh University. Conan-Doyle wrote 60 adventures in total. The collection is known as *The Cannon*. All but 4 stories are narrated by Holmes' loyal sidekick Dr Watson. Together, they solve the most amazing mysteries. Now think for a moment. What's the most famous Sherlock Holmes expression you know?

Most probably you answered, "Elementary, my dear Watson." Now here's the interesting part. The character Sherlock Holmes never actually uses this precise phrase. You won't find it in any of Conan-Doyle's books. Holmes does say 'Watson' all the time. He was his loyal companion after all. He also uses the word 'elementary' repeatedly, as a way of showing how smart he is. *(They run into the most complex situations. Holmes points out the solution and states it's 'elementary' as if the solution is the most obvious thing in the world).* And somehow, both words ended up together. Why? Because there's a nice fit. We can easily imagine Sherlock Holmes saying, "Elementary, my dear Watson," showing his unique ability and intellectual superiority towards his friend Watson. It's a characteristic of a communication phenomenon science calls *Message Distortion,* another villain on the execution road. It explains part of my mystery. Both topics, the tipping point and the Rule of 150 are present in Gladwell's book. The first is the main concept and book title. The second is part of the conditions to reach a tipping point. So they're closely related, but not linked together, just like 'elementary' and 'my dear Watson'. To the casual listener who hears, "You need to get 150 people behind your idea to reach the tipping point", it sounds perfectly plausible and therefore doesn't get more consideration. *(What did you think when you read the idea at the start of this chapter?).* And so the tipping point and the Rule of 150 become entwined.

To solve the rest of the puzzle, let's study a second transmission problem. It appears that the more messages are passed on, the *shorter* they get. And this editing process is much more dramatic than most of us realise. Gordon Allport and Joseph Postman researched message shortening. And their results are astonishing.

A message loses a whopping 70 percent of its details after 5 to 6 mouth-to-mouth transmissions. Let's take a closer look. Gladwell provides 3 tactics to reach a tipping point and create a word-of-mouth epidemic: (1) We should focus our resources on a few key groups—Connectors, Mavens, and Salesmen; (2) We should make our message sticky and; (3) We should structure the environment to our advantage. To support the third point, Gladwell talks about the 150 dynamic. He

argues that if you can launch your idea in a small group where everyone knows each other, you idea will spread faster. *(Just think about
the gossiping in small villages compared to next-door neighbors in big
cities who never speak to each other).* Of all the tips he proposes, the
Rule of 150 is the most attractive to use in communication. Why? Because it's easy to see a tipping point as a scale. You turn the volume
up to above 150 and it tips. And getting 150 people behind our great
idea is something we could all achieve. It's not that many people. And
that makes the message very attractive to share. *(Sharing an unknown,
easy tip makes the narrator popular).*

2.
Strategy Graffiti

People shorten *and* package messages. This explains how the tipping
point becomes *the tripping point.* But Message Distortion doesn't limit itself to individuals sharing ideas they pick up from a favorite book.
Message Distortion happens *all the time,* even when lives are at stake.
Take a look at this string of commands from the US Army 1st Air Caval-
ry Division. It happened during the Vietnam War in 1967. In this tragic
example, people died because the core of the message—do *not* burn
the hamlet (small village)—got lost in the communication cascade.

> Divisional headquarters communicated to the brigade: "On no
> occasions must hamlets be burned down."

> The brigade radioed the battalion: "Do not burn down any
> hamlets unless you are absolutely convinced the Viet Cong are
> in them."

> The battalion radioed the infantry company at the scene: "If
> you think there are any Viet Cong in the hamlet, burn it down."

The company commander ordered his troops: "Burn down that hamlet."

It doesn't come as a surprise that our strategy—or to be precise, our strategy story—also distorts. When people talk about strategy and the strategy message gets passed along, parts of it are left out and bits and pieces get packaged in the wrong order. The name given to this phenomenon is *Strategy Graffiti.* Let's be clear. When the strategy storyline is passed from one individual to another, there's *always* going to be a certain amount of Strategy Graffiti that ends up on our message. We have seen that even with the best possible formulation—few strategies are summarized as clearly as Malcolm Gladwell's ideas—messages become distorted when passed along. So the key question becomes, "If it happens all the time, should we care?" In other words, do strategists need to care about the villain Message Distortion? The answer: when Strategy Graffiti hides the core of our big idea, we should care.

3.
A Horse is Not a Zebra

Running a successful zoo was getting more and more challenging. Marc Williams, CEO of The Mighty Beast, the seventh largest zoo in the world, was fidgeting anxiously in his chair. He had seen the quarterly results yesterday and that was it. He had to take action and push his plan forwards. Today, he decided, he was going to hire a strategy consulting company to screen the company and propose a new strategy. He would go for The Chicago Consulting Group because one of the partners was a close friend of Peter Marchal, chairman of the zoo's board. He was convinced that this little edge would play in his favor when the results were presented.

Four months later, Marc was sitting in his office happily enjoying his success. The strategy presentation to the board had gone as planned that morning. They'd praised him for it, even though he'd had little to do with the end result. "And now it's time for the others to do some work," he said to himself while calling out for Daniel, his operations manager.

Daniel Brown wasn't surprised to be summoned to Marc's office again. It was a regular occurrence. And he could never guess the reason as his boss had a tendency to interpret an ops manager's job description in various ways. Today was no different. Before he had a chance to sit down, Marc told him, "Daniel, I want you to communicate the strategy that I have developed to everyone in our company." "You know Daniel," Marc continued, "Hoofed animals are great animals. So I have decided to have more of them in our zoo." The strategy consultants had recommended that visitors should be encouraged to return to the zoo more often to stimulate the much-needed sales of annual subscriptions. One suggestion was to have some domesticated animals like horses. This would give the opportunity for increased animal-human interaction and the chance for people to bond with the animals. If horses were kept near the zoo entrance, people could also take chariot tours. Children and grandparents alike would love it. But Marc wanted to keep things simple for Daniel. So he only gave him the basic information.

Daniel didn't think much of the idea. But he was happy to be Marc's strategy spokesperson. He didn't care too much about what he needed to say, as long as his job was secure. And he couldn't see how getting some extra animals could negatively affect his position.

The first person Daniel spoke to was finance manager Debra Winger. Halfway through his second coffee, he said to her: "Marc has decided to increase the number of hoofed animals in our zoo. And he's asked me to tell everyone about it." Debra thought Marc's idea was great. A larger herd of zebras would provide for a better breeding program and increase the zoo's status. She was also very fond of the gracious striped animals.

After the meeting, Debra called purchasing manager Paul Yuzinsky: "Marc wants you to order 7 more zebras ASAP." So Paul did exactly as he was told. Questioning his boss wasn't part of his job description. He went to buy 7 zebras. The price was steep as the only zoo willing to sell them at such short notice was the Central Zoo, 2,200 miles away.

Marianne Brenner, the keeper in charge of zebras, was surprised when she got a phone call telling her to unload 2 trucks with 7 zebras. "Buying more zebras is such a stupid move," she thought. They already had a nice herd and a top-notch breeding program. "We should be selling zebras, not buying them."

Marc looked out of his office window to see the 2 white trucks arriving with what looked like horses. He couldn't see properly as the unloading area was on the other side of the zoo. "That was quick," he thought. For once, he decided to show his appreciation and asked his secretary to call the person in charge.

Marianne answered the phone and listened to Marc's praise. "Too bad we didn't get any horses," she thought. "It's not really a zoo animal, but we could use them to take visitors around. That would really boost our visitor numbers." But since Marc and his fancy consultants were paid to do the thinking, she let it go and went off to unload the zebras.

■ ■ ■

When I'm on stage, I love to use this story to animate a discussion on Message Distortion. When a strategy story travels, it gets sprayed with Strategy Graffiti. Stripes are added to the horse. As we've learned, that happens all the time. It's part of how people communicate. And as long as the horse stays a horse with a few stripes, we're fine. But when the horse turns into a zebra, our big idea is in trouble.

Marketers face the same challenge. They have a brand (the horse) that needs to be kept stripe-free. Marketers call this 'protecting the brand essence'. "It's very important to safeguard the core claim of the brand," Nico Croes, senior marketeer at BBDO, one of the world's largest marketing agencies, told me. "Each brand has an identity, something it stands for. And it's crucial customers recognize the core. It's what sets it apart from the competing products or services. When we advertise, we need to make sure the core of the brand message remains intact. If it doesn't, we have a big problem." Think about the following 2 examples. Can you spot the communication cascade with a graffiti problem?

Example 1

CEO to N-1: In order to survive in our industry, we need to tap into new profit pools. This demands a new client attitude. But if we don't keep our costs under control, we won't be in the game at all. So we need even more efficiency gains.

N-1 to N-2: We have to grow our business and therefore need more satisfied customers. We also need to keep our costs under control in order to survive.

N-2 to Lisa: We need to increase customer satisfaction and become more efficient.

Example 2

CEO to N-1: In order to survive in our industry, we need to tap into new profit pools. This demands a new client attitude. But, if we don't keep our costs under control, we won't be in the game at all. This requires even more efficiency gains.

N-1 to N-2: It's crucial to become more client-oriented. It will secure our long-term. But we cannot drop the ball in the short-term. Always focus on costs.

N-3 to Lisa: Focus on efficiency first, be customer-oriented where possible.

The answer, of course, is number 1. While both messages end up distorted, the core remains intact in the second. In the first example, the message distorts to the extent that the core idea—to keep costs down and use the savings to prepare for the future—is lost. It's not clear any more that efficiency comes first.

Now here's the scary part. Someone who knows the strategy *(remember the Tapper?)* doesn't pay attention to the crucial difference. Why? Because of the Curse of Knowledge. He already knows the core message. He hears the song, even if most notes are missing. When you know that your company competes in a declining industry, you know it's important to look for new profit pools. You also know that finding them takes time. And it's evident the current business provides the cash to bridge the gap. That's the tune that will automatically play in your head when you hear the notes 'efficiency' and 'customer service'. Knowing the context, it's easy to prioritize, even if you only hear 2 words. Efficiency comes first.

For a Listener like Lisa and someone who doesn't have the context, customer satisfaction and efficiency have equal value. And with the information given by the executive in the first example, Lisa can't prioritize. She's unable to see the decision pattern so doesn't know how to stay on the right path. But with the information from the executive in the second example, she can.

4.
Distortion TV

Just like successful brand managers safeguard the core of the brand—the brand essence, successful strategists safeguard the core of the strategy—the big choice. Our first job is to make the villain Message Distortion visible. One of the most effective ways of doing this in a large organization is to make a video. Here's how it works. Get yourself a TV crew for a day—nothing fancy, just 1 or 2 people and an amateur video camera. Go to every corner of the organization and ask 40-50 people to tell the strategy story. Ask them, for example, "What are the 3 most important things for our company to succeed?" Once you've collected enough material, cut and paste it into one video. Bring the senior team around the table, watch it, and discuss the outcome.

It's good to know that most organizations have similar graffiti problems. When analyzing the results, look for the following 2 patterns. First of all, from a structure perspective, Strategy Graffiti will be more dominant in certain groups of the company such as teams, business areas, departments or countries. *(Some got the message, others didn't)*. Secondly, from a content perspective, Strategy Graffiti will be more dominant on some parts of the strategy message than others. *(Some parts of the strategy message survived the communication cascade, others didn't)*.

Let's go back to the Gladwell mystery and see if we can judge the impact of the villain Message Distortion. How would you evaluate its effect on Gladwell's big idea? In my opinion, the core of the message is clearly touched. Gladwell's idea is in trouble. First of all, parts of the core message are left out. When I want to create a tipping point, I don't have all the information to make the right decisions. Crucial elements like the importance of focus on a few key groups—the Mavens, Connectors, and Salesmen—and the need to craft a sticky message, are missing. Secondly, the tipping point, as explained by the 5 people, becomes a dangerous mathematical formula. Imagine that you and I, those 5 people, and a bunch of others, all work for the same company. And Malcolm Gladwell is our CEO. Imagine also that the Rule of 150 is a crucial element of our company strategy. Instead of making small decisions to keep groups *below* 150, we get the advice from our colleagues to push the group size *over* 150. Exactly the opposite of what we should be doing, according to our CEO. And the wrong message isn't contained. It keeps spreading, like a virus.

CHAPTER 4

Draw
a Finish Line

My son Jonas is 8. He's really into soccer. He plays in the local little league and is constantly asking every family member to play soccer with him in the garden. When I'm not traveling, I end up in the garden pretty much every day.

Before we start, he always gives me 2 options: "Do we play for real?" *(a match)* or "Do we practice?" In theory, the game we play is exactly the same—the only difference being that when we play for real, we keep score. But this slight variation makes a huge difference to the way Jonas approaches the game. He's at his best when he's 1 or 2 goals behind. He then plays with drive, takes calculated risks, runs a lot, and challenges pretty much every goal I take. Keeping the score also influences my behavior. While I don't mind him winning the game, if I'm honest, I prefer a tight game or I won't hear the end of it until we play again. So whenever I'm behind by more than 3 or 4 goals, I push a little harder to limit the loss *(as long as he's 8, I'm still able to do so)*.

But here's the thing. Why do we take a game more seriously when we state upfront that it's 'for real'? We're really playing exactly the same game with the same people. So why does something as seemingly insignificant as counting goals have such a big impact on our behavior?

1.
Who's Winning?

In 1990, Professor Edwin Locke and Gary Latham published *A Theory of Goal-setting & Task Performance*, a groundbreaking study based on 400 laboratory and field experiments carried out over 25 years. Their research provides 2 important insights for our journey. First of all, when we define goals, we perform better than when we don't. Both professors argue that by setting goals, we create a standard for self-satisfaction with performance. In other words, by telling ourselves what success looks like, we want to chase it and be successful. Secondly, regular feedback on our progress towards our chosen goal boosts our performance. Latham and Locke point out that regular feedback improves our decision-making and problem-solving abilities. By tracking our progress and knowing where we stand, we adapt our efforts and techniques to make sure we reach our goal. That's exactly what happens when my son and I play soccer 'for real'. There is a clear goal—my son wants to win and I don't want to lose with a big goal difference. We can both keep track of where we stand as there's immediate feedback *(my son reminds me of the score every few minutes)*. And we both dig a bit deeper to reach our goal.

Latham and Locke proved with their revolutionary research that keeping the score is one of the most powerful performance mechanisms. If we're serious about strategy execution performance, we need a clear goal and a feedback mechanism that tells us exactly where we are and where we should be. But finding the right feedback mechanisms on our strategy journey can be quite a challenge and even a bit tricky. The easiest way is to work backwards. So let's start by drawing a finish line.

2.
Are We There Yet?

A few years ago, 28-year-old Jef Schrauwen got a challenging request. He was asked to take over the family business and step into the footsteps of 6 generations of carpenters.

Before making such an important decision, Jef decided to evaluate the company's potential. The financial results weren't bad. But as he expected, there was a clear downward trend. Competition was fierce, margins eroding. Their product portfolio was quite diverse, ranging from windows and window shutters to exterior doors, and even a few pool houses. Their passion for quality craftsmanship was obvious. And everyone, including himself, was proud of their 123-year history.

Jef concluded that the only way forwards was to focus on a higher added-value product with a decent margin where craftsmanship still made a difference. He decided to specialize in high-quality front doors for classic townhouses and villas. To answer the needs of demanding homeowners, he knew he had to combine craftsmanship with the increasing demands for modern comfort, safety, and energy preservation.

Once he was convinced that he'd identified a future for the company, he accepted the challenge and started sharing his big idea with others. He talked enthusiastically about front doors and the opportunity it presented for their company. But, to his dismay, he just got difficult questions and apathy in return. Jef Schrauwen wondered why others didn't see the future in the same way he did.

Today, Atelier Schrauwen is a very successful company that specializes in exclusive front doors. It combines old charm with modern production techniques. Their employees rave enthusiastically about their product and service. Owner Jef is renowned as a very successful entrepreneur. He won the national craftsmanship award and was praised for his bold move. His approach to strategy is now used as a 'how to' for others.

So what happened? Did Jef get lucky or was there something else?

Here's how Jef formulates his breakthrough: "When I was asked to take over the family business, I thought the most difficult step would be to define a great future for the company. I didn't want to be the one who messed up the family history. But, in hindsight, the real challenge was to get the others behind my dream. At the beginning, they didn't share my enthusiasm and talking about it didn't seem to help. On the contrary, they'd say things like "We're doing well today," "Our order book is full for several months ahead," or, "Why should we focus on one product only?" After months of struggling, I took a different approach and decided to quantify my dream. I came up with the following statement: "By 2017, we want to be producing 200 top-quality front doors per year." This little phrase made quite a difference to the team. They're quite competitive and started counting and figuring out if we were making progress or not. The slogan also proved to be very effective to the outside world. Clients, prospects, and the media got behind it and involved themselves into our story."

By adding a *finish line*, Jef made strategy success tangible for everyone. He didn't change his big choice—to become the specialist in exclusive front doors. But the finish line—to produce and sell 200 doors a year—showed everyone involved what winning would look like, just like goal counting does to a soccer game. By picking a finish line for the strategy, successful strategists show what success looks like. They define clear rules on how to win and turn an abstract idea into a concrete race.

3.
Motivation

A finish line shows what strategy success looks like. But as we learn from Jef's experience, the right finish line also motivates. It gives purpose to those traveling the execution road. And we've learned from Latham and Locke that having a clear goal—a purpose—increases performance. It triggers our desire to win. So we don't just want *any* finish line. We want an *inspiring* finish line.

Many organizations have defined a finish line for their strategy, but it lacks inspiration. Take this example. While some might get a kick out of, "We want to outperform the market and have a ROCE of at least 2 percent higher than the industry average in the next 5 years," the reality is that most people just don't care. Another wonderful example of the impact of an inspiring finish line is NASA. Here's what they aspired to in the early 60's.

> The expansion of human knowledge of phenomena in the atmosphere and space; the improvement of the usefulness, performance, speed, safety, and efficiency of aeronautical and space vehicles; the development and operation of vehicles capable of carrying instruments, equipment, supplies, and living organisms through space; the establishment of long-range studies of the potential benefits to be gained from, the opportunities for, and the problems involved in the utilization of aeronautical and space activities for peaceful and scientific purposes; the preservation of the role of the United States as a leader in aeronautical and space science and technology and in the application

thereof to the conduct of peaceful activities within and outside the atmosphere; the making available to agencies directly concerned with national defense of discoveries that have military value or significance, and the furnishing by such agencies, to the civilian agency established to direct and control nonmilitary aeronautical and space activities, of information as to discoveries which have value or significance to that agency; cooperation by the United States with other nations and groups of nations in work done pursuant to this Act and in the peaceful application of the results thereof; the most effective utilization of the scientific and engineering resources of the United States, with close cooperation among all interested agencies of the United States in order to avoid unnecessary duplication of effort, facilities and equipment.

Excited yet? Probably not. But then a brilliant communicator added the following finish line: "I believe that this nation should commit itself to achieving the goal, before this decade is out, of landing a man on the moon and returning him safely to the earth." At the time, John F. Kennedy's finish line inspired an entire nation.

4.
NASA's Not So Bold Move

We can learn a second lesson from NASA's example, a crucial insight that might surprise you. The finish line that John F. Kennedy formulated was *not* a bold statement. While going to the moon in the 60's sounded like science fiction to most people, it didn't for NASA. Going to the moon was quite a realistic finish line, based on the core of NASA's strategy at the time. Here's how former NASA employee and well-known strategist Richard Rumelt judges the reality of NASA's finish line: "The objective Kennedy set, seemingly audacious to the layman, was quite proximate. It was a matter of marshaling the resources and political will. The objective was feasible because engineers knew how to design and build rockets and spacecraft. Much of the technology had already been developed as part of the ballistic missile program."

While Jef's finish line—200 doors by 2017—is tough, it's also realistic. "The number 200 isn't a wild guess, even taking into account that we only produced 25 doors a year at the time I came up with the statement," Jef told me. "It was based on our maximum production capacity. At the time, our major challenge was to shift our product portfolio. I calculated how many doors we would be able to produce if we would focus only on front doors, stopping all other products. The number happened to be 200."

Both examples teach us the importance of a realistic link between the strategy—the big choice—and the finish line. You don't pick a *random* finish line, one that competitor's use, or that business schools illustrate in a case study, or one that simply sounds impressive. You pick a finish line that *captures the core* of your strategy and provides a *tough, but realistic challenge*. A finish line isn't a daydream—like winning the lottery jackpot one day. A finish line is a statement that starts from the realistic potential. Jef's finish line was realistic because he had the production capacity. As was NASA's finish line because they had the technology. Michael Phelps finish line—to become the greatest Olympian that's ever lived—is a daydream for 7 billion people, but it wasn't for him. He knew he had the capabilities to pull it off. And it probably inspired him to dive into the pool day after day. Successful strategists choose a challenging, but realistic finish line that captures the strategy core. And by doing so, we inspire travelers. We give purpose to the strategy journey—just like goal counting does to a father and son playing soccer in their backyard.

CHAPTER 5

Re-measure

A finish line tells us when our strategy journey is successfully completed. It tells us when we won. An inspiring finish line, such as JFK's 'man on the moon by the end of the century' and Jef's '200 front doors by 2017', gives everyone involved purpose. It motivates us to win. But a finish line doesn't tell us how to complete the journey successfully. It doesn't tell us how to win. Therefore, we need a second item to complete our feedback mechanism. We need a set of signposts that point us towards the finish line. To find our second indicator set, let's take a look at the decisions successful marathon runners make to improve their personal best on this mythical running distance.

The marathon commemorates Pheidippides, a soldier who ran from a battlefield in the Greek town of Marathon to Athens in 490BC.

He was to deliver news of the Greek victory over the Persians. Legend has it that Pheidippides delivered the momentous message "NIKI" *(meaning 'victory')* and then collapsed and died. When the modern Olympic Games were inaugurated in 1896 in Greece, Pheidippides was honored with a 24.85-mile run from Marathon Bridge to the Olympic stadium in Athens. At the 1908 Olympic Games in London, the marathon distance was changed to 26.2 miles to cover the distance from White City Stadium to Windsor Castle so the race would end in front of the Royal Family's viewing box. *(That's why some runners today shout "God Save the Queen!" at milepost 24)*. After 16 years of heated discussion, the official finish line was established at 26.2 miles.

For most runners, crossing the finish line of a marathon is a dream come true, a once-in-a-lifetime achievement. But for a select group of runners, the finish line is business-as-usual and should be reached as fast as possible. Professional marathon runners compete to win.

The number of competitions that these athletes enter each year is limited. Not because they don't want to, but because of the immense physical impact of such a race. "A marathon has a grueling impact on your body, even if you're a professional athlete", marathon coach Tomás Valcke told me while recovering from his last marathon. "Researchers followed a group of runners and drew blood on a daily basis after the race. It took a month for the blood levels to get back to normal. Our body needs at least a month to recover from a marathon. And from a training perspective, the impact has an even longer effect. Amateur runners often think they can run a second marathon after a month and improve their time. But that's not how our body works. A race puts you back—your pre-race condition *(the speed at which you can run a certain distance)* is gone. You have to rebuild your race speed, which takes a few months. Only then, can you repeat the same performance or try to do better."

As marathon runners only run a few races a year, they have limited feedback from competitions to improve their performance. Therefore, they've always been looking for ways to perform better by *predicting* their finish line success. So how do they do it? How do marathon runners predict finish line success without actually having to run 26.2 miles?

1.
Yasso 800

The first predictor they use is the average number of miles they run per week. There happens to be a strong correlation between the weekly miles an athlete runs and the time on the next marathon. Valcke confirms this. "When I coach runners with a personal best of 3.05 hours, with an ambition to dive under the magic 3-hour limit, we first check if their body balance is optimal. *(Can this runner lose weight without losing speed?)*. But often, with a personal best of close to 3 hours, there's not much room for improvement. You won't find many overweight runners crossing the finish line after 3 hours. So we try to increase the number of training miles per week to the 55-65 range. Research proves that, on average, the more miles you run a week, the better your time at the next marathon." But as with weight, the second indicator has its limits. Why? Because the more miles you run a week, the higher the risk of injury. "There's always a risk of overtraining," Valcke says. "Each person is different so there's no optimal number. It's about trial and error to find the balance."

Then Bart Yasso came up with a surprising third indicator: "The time it takes you to run 800-meter *(2 laps)* repeats in minutes and seconds works out to be your marathon finish time in hours and minutes." How does it work? The theory behind the Yasso 800 is that your time in minutes and seconds for a workout of 10 times 800 meters with equal recovery time, is the same as the hours and minutes of your marathon time. For example, if you can run 10 times 800 meters in 3 minutes and 20 seconds with 3 minutes and 20 seconds of recovery, this predicts that you can run 3 hours and 20 minutes for your marathon. Run 2:50 for the 800's and you can run 2:50 for the marathon. "The Yasso 800 is a well-known, but very challenging interval training," Valcke points out, "and, on average, it does predict your marathon time quite accurately. I've tried it, as have several of the runners I coach."

I realize it's quite counter-intuitive when you hear this for the first time. How can the time of a distance that's less than 2 percent of the total distance predict success? Pretty crazy, isn't it? But the simple truth is that it's quite accurate. Extensive tests have proved that the time for the 800 meters is one of the best marathon time predictors. Improving your time on the 800 meters means improving your time on the marathon. The Yasso 800 helps marathon runners predict success—and with great accuracy.

■ ■ ■

The finish line of a marathon—just like the finish line of our strategy journey—is a *lag* indicator. It's called this because the measurement lags behind the result. By the time you get the data—your time at the finish line—the result has happened. A marathon runner who crossed the finish line will see the result, but it's too late to change it. The race is over.

The Yasso 800 is a *lead* indicator. It's called this because the measurement leads to the result. By the time you get the data *(your Yasso 800 time)*, the result *(your marathon success)* still has to happen. The great thing about lead indicators is that they offer direction on *how* to improve performance. They offer users the possibility to predict success *and* make decisions to positively influence success. A marathon runner who runs the Yasso 800 will find out what her time will look like at the finish line. If it's not as desired, she adjusts her training program and improves before the actual race.

Like marathon runners, travelers also need a limited set of lead indicators— signposts—that predict success at the finish line. This feedback mechanism helps them make the right decisions along the way. Finding the right set is something of an art form that requires trial and error to get it right. At the start, it feels like playing roulette. But over time, with patience and practice, the odds will turn in your favor. And when that happens, it's a real game changer. When you discover a signpost others missed, just like Billy Beane did, you hit the jackpot.

2.
Billy Beane

What do you do if your team is on a losing streak and you don't have the money to try and buy yourself a way out? That's what Billy Beane was facing. In the 90's, he was the struggling general manager of the Oakland Athletics baseball team—or 'the A's' as they are commonly known. The team was in a lose-lose situation with no hope of a turnaround in sight. Like other big hitters in the League, they didn't have the financial means to buy themselves out of the hole they were in. They were one of the poorest teams in Major League Baseball with one-fifth of the budget of wealthy teams for new players, a crumbling stadium, and collapsing attendance figures. Billy Beane had to find a way to save the team. And fast.

He decided to focus on what produces baseball wins. After all, winning is all anyone cares about. He started with the premise that the highest number of runs produces wins. But what contributes to these wins? What are the lead measures that create a run? The traditional view of team selection was based on experienced scouts analyzing a player's technical capability—like how they batted and ran between bases—as well as how physically attractive they *(and even their girl-friends)* were. Billy Beane went against the tide. With the help of computer whiz Paul DePodesta, they set out to challenge the conventions of baseball. The duo believed that the players' statistical records *(the lead indicators)* mattered more than their technical abilities. And, with this in mind, they recruited a list of 'nobodies'—awkward has-been players who could do one thing really well and really consistently... they could get on base.

"It's about getting things down to one number. Using stats to re-read them, we'll find the value of players that no one else can see," says Paul DePodesta's character in the film *Moneyball*. "Baseball thinking is medieval. They're asking all the wrong questions and, if I say it to any-body, I'm ostracized. I'm a rebel. I believe that there's a championship team of 25 people that we can afford. Because everyone else in base-ball undervalues them. Like an island of misfit toys."

For a while, these misfits were a laughing stock... that is until they started winning games again. They won the division title, beating teams way richer in talent and money. During the next decade, they al-ways ended up first or second in their division. Since then, the impact of 'sabermetrics'—the analysis of baseball through statistics—and the focus on non-traditional indicators has become common practice in major league baseball. "To me, it was taking a critical eye to everything you do and being vigilant in the process, reassessing, challenging as-sumptions and constraints to find a way that works for you," says Paul DePodesta, "and I see that everywhere, not just in baseball."

3.
Remove Old Signposts

Like every road, the execution shortcut needs maintenance. Signposts that confuse the traveler should be removed. But for some reason, people find it hard to remove old indicators. They seem to have a particular magic about them. We find it very difficult to let them go—just like the magic ring that Frodo has to destroy. Why? Because it turns out that information is addictive. And addicts find it hard to let go.

Dr Hallowell, an associate professor at Harvard and John Ratey, a psychiatrist specializing in Attention Deficit Disorder (ADD), point out that people can get compulsively drawn to the constant stimulation of incoming data. "It's magnetic," says Edward Hallowell. Both scientists have their own term for this condition—'pseudo-ADD'. Its sufferers do not actually have Attention Deficit Disorder, but, influenced by technology and the pace of modern life, have developed shorter attention spans. They become frustrated with long-term projects and thrive on the stress of constant fixes of information. And that's because information hits our dopamine receptors, just like drugs and alcohol.

One of the results of our information addiction is an overload of indicators, all collected in a nice-looking dashboard. There's nothing better to feed our information craving than a set of fancy spreadsheets and a ton of complicated indicators. But big dashboards can be quite hazardous on our strategy journey. They can slow down the decision process, like having too many jars of jam to choose from at the grocery store. With too many indicators, it becomes difficult for travelers to choose a path. *(Which signpost should I follow?)*. Big dashboards can also create a false sense of ok. It's the, "All traffic lights are green and so all is fine" attitude. And they also heavily impact on workload. A simple-looking indicator with a single target figure might demand a week's work to collect the data. Sometimes it's tough, but often it's not because data collection is scattered. Consider approving a simple measurement action that demands 'only an hour of each employee every quarter' in a company of 1,000 employees. You just approved 2.6 full-time equivalents!

To evaluate the added value of an indicator, we should ask ourselves: "What important decision does this measure help us make?" The word 'important' is important. It's tempting to answer 'yes' *(remember the dopamine hit)*, but it's a question of *how important*. It's like the temperature indicator you see on an airplane's onboard TV. It's cool to know it's extremely cold outside, but it won't get you any faster to your destination. Or think about the tachometer on the dashboard of a fancy car. This indicator shows the engine rotation rate, typically with markings indicating the safe range. They're cool to look at when you fire away, but you don't need them to know when to shift gears as the sound of your engine will tell you that *(and those who do maybe shouldn't be driving a manual car)*.

4.
Players Versus Coach

A second crucial element to avoid information overload is to distinguish between the information needs of the coach and those of the players. The authors of *The 4 Disciplines of Execution* say of the coaching scoreboard:

> Visually displaying data is not new to you or your team. In fact, you may be thinking that you already have a scoreboard, or even lots of scoreboards, all captured in complex spreadsheets inside your computer. And the data just keeps coming in. Most of this data is in the form of lag measures accompanied by historical trends, forward projections, and financial analysis. The data

is important and it serves a purpose for you as a leader; your spreadsheets are what we would call a coach's scoreboard… To drive execution you need a player's scoreboard that has a few simple graphs on it indicating: Here's where we need to be and here's where we are right now. In 5 seconds or less, anyone can determine whether we are winning or losing.

In other words, the coaching dashboard is the easy part. Our focus should be on the players' scoreboard. For our journey, we need to build a simple dashboard for our travelers—a dashboard that visualizes the finish line and the signposts, the lead indicators that predict success at the finish line. As you know, not every player contributes to success in the same way. In football, the defense has a different role to the offense. In soccer, the keeper is different to the field players. In baseball, the pitcher is different to the fielding team. We therefore need several smaller player dashboards, each adapted to the specific role of each group of travelers. In an organization, for example, sales reps and operations share the same finish line, but have a different set of signposts.

SO FAR, we've learned a great deal about successful strategy journeys. We know how great strategy journeys start—with a big choice, a decision regarding the client segment *(the 'who')*, and the value chain *(the 'how')*. And we know how great strategy journeys end—with a finish line, a destination postcard that captures the core of the big choice and shows travelers in an inspiring way what strategy success looks like.

In between the start and finish, we've learned that day-to-day decisions play a key role. These SMALL choices need to be in line with the big choice to create a path, a Mintzberg Pattern. Successful strategists facilitate these small choices using 3 tactics: (1) They provide a List of

Noes to limit the options, just like Michael Porter taught us; (2) They provide prioritization information—a Decision Intent—for the remaining options, just like Alexandre Behring's did with his 5 simple rules; and (3) They keep the core of the strategy clearly visible—free from Strategy Graffiti—just like brand managers who protect their brand.

We've also learned that having a goal and matching feedback mechanism is crucial. A finish line tells us *when* we are successful and motivates travelers, just like Jef's slogan did for a group of craftsmen and JFK's line did for an entire nation. Signposts tell us *how* to be successful, just like the Yasso 800 does for a marathon runner and sabermetrics do for a baseball coach. The right set of signposts can make all the difference in the world. If only we can overcome our information addiction and focus on the traveler.

The key question for the second part of our journey is whether we can connect our big idea with the hearts of the travelers on the execution road. Can we learn how to make others *care* about our big idea? I think we can.

PART 2

HEART

CHAPTER 6

Share Strategy Stories

D ave, a friend of a friend, is a frequent business traveler. He was recently in Atlantic City for an important client meeting. He had some time to kill before his return flight and went to a local bar for a drink.

He'd just finished one drink when an attractive woman approached and asked if she could buy him another. He was surprised, but flattered. "Sure" he replied. The woman walked back to the bar and brought over 2 more drinks—one for her and the other for him. He thanked her and took a sip. And that was the last thing he remembered before waking up in a hotel bathtub, his body submerged in ice.

He looked around, frantically trying to figure out where he was and how he'd got there. Then he spotted the note: "DON'T MOVE. CALL 911."

A cell phone lay on a small table beside the bathtub. He picked it up and called 911, his fingers numb and clumsy from the ice. The operator seemed strangely familiar with his situation. She said, "Sir, I want you to reach behind you, slowly and carefully. Is there a tube protruding from your lower back?"

Anxiously, he felt around his back. Sure enough, there was a tube.

The operator said, "Sir, don't panic, but one of your kidneys has been harvested. There's a ring of organ thieves operating in this city and they have got to you. Paramedics are on their way. Don't move until they arrive."

1.
Strategy Stickiness

You've just read the Kidney Heist, a famous urban legend. Dan and Chip Heath recount this colorful myth at the start of their excellent book *Made to Stick*. They continue by contrasting the story with a statement that sounds very much like the boring phrase you came across in Chapter 4—we want to outperform the market and have a ROCE that is at least 2 percent higher than the market average in the chosen time period of our strategy plan. They then challenge the reader to put the book aside, wait an hour, call a friend and recount both stories to see how much they remember.

Unsurprisingly, the Kidney Heist story wins. "A story is powerful because it provides context missing from abstract prose," the Heath brothers point out. "Stories put knowledge into a framework that is more lifelike, more true to our day-to-day existence." In other words, the right story wrapped around an idea makes the core message stickier—easier to remember. Psychologist Jerome Bruner quantified story stickiness. He concluded that facts are 20 times more likely to be remembered if they're part of a story. This insight is very interesting for strategists as we want travelers to remember our strategy message on the execution road. We want our idea to stick, just like the Kidney

Heist story.

When employees complain about the quality of communication, they say things like "The strategy is not clear" or "Our organization doesn't have a strategy." But the underlying point they want to make is, "I'm unable to put the information I got in a context that makes sense to me." *I don't see what kind of small choices I have to make to contribute to the big choice.*

Most idea creators don't pay attention to this second hidden message. And that's because of the villain, the Curse of Knowledge. Remember the tapping experiment? Once people know something, they find it very hard to put themselves in the shoes of those that don't. When executives hear comments on their strategy communication, they're oblivious to the fact that others find it hard to apply the message to their world. They mistakenly think listeners didn't hear the message and, to succeed, repetition is needed. They think, "Let's do another roadshow or write another newsletter article." It's like foreigners who repeat their message louder and more slowly when they see that you didn't get the point they want to make. But the frown on your forehead didn't mean, "I didn't *hear* your message," but rather "I heard the message but I don't *get it*." *(I hear the Chinese words you're speaking, but since I don't understand Chinese, I have no clue what you're saying. And slowly repeating the message in Chinese isn't going to help me understand it any better).* Repetition doesn't outwit the Curse of Knowledge. Stories do. Why? Because stories offer listeners crucial message context. They offer additional information helping listeners to frame the facts in a setting that makes sense to them.

2.
The Story That Changed the World Bank

Stephen Denning was on his way to the top. A bright executive running a large chunk of the World Bank's operations, Denning loved his job. He enjoyed traveling to remote countries, dealing with clients, and solving their problems. But then he got a 'promotion'. Denning was asked to look into the issue of knowledge management at the World Bank. He wasn't happy. "Why should I leave this exciting world and look into the unglamorous issue of information?" he asked himself after getting the offer. At the time, managing information was low priority at the World Bank. And with it came a matching low status job. A shift from operations to information was like a chef in a top restaurant being 'promoted' to a job in which he needed to organize the dishwasher. He knew the move wouldn't help his career.

But Denning believed in the power of knowledge management. "As an early advocate of personal computing who had felt the exhilaration and liberation that it offered, I had some inkling of the potential." So he knew that, if he succeeded, the benefits for the World Bank would be enormous. He just had to find a way to show his colleagues the potential of the idea. After careful deliberation, Stephen Denning decided to accept the challenge.

But it didn't work out as he'd hoped. Denning remembers prowling the company corridors and canteen looking for people to convince. He would invite them to his office, explaining the importance of knowledge management. Or, if that didn't work, try to persuade them on the spot. Progress was slow and painful. "I found it difficult to get anyone to listen," he recalls. "Most of the people couldn't or wouldn't understand an idea that seemed so obvious and logical to me."

And with every argument he made, he got 2 counter arguments in return. "To them, the notion (of knowledge management) was strange," Denning said. But then, somehow, it made it onto the agenda of a global senior management meeting. But his initial excitement quickly evaporated when he saw the schedule. "I was dismayed. A mere half-hour was allocated. And worse still, 2 other speakers were fitted into the same time slot." This left him with just 10 minutes to convince the audience. An impossible challenge. In the end, Denning took a last minute-gamble and adopted a totally different approach. Instead of building an argument, he decided to tell a story:

In June 1995, a health worker in a tiny town in Zambia went to the website of the Centers for Disease Control (CDC) and got the answer to a question about the treatment of malaria. Remember this was in Zambia—one of the poorest countries in the world—in a tiny place 375 miles from the capital city. But the most striking thing about this picture, at least for us, is that the World Bank isn't in it. Despite our know-how on all kinds of poverty-related issues, that knowledge isn't available to the millions of people who could use it. Imagine if it were. Think what an organization we could become!

While on stage, he noticed positive body language from the audience. He sensed that he had them gripped. And when he'd finished, instead of the usual, "This will never work for us" and "It doesn't fit our business," he got a very different reaction. The audience asked, "Why don't we do it?" Here's how Denning recalls the discussion that followed:

I say that we have to persuade the whole organization to accept the strategy and that not everyone is yet a believer. "Why not?" they persist excitedly. "What's the blockage?"
The element that seems slightly strange about these exchanges is that the questions are framed as if it's their idea being dis-

cussed and not mine. They're speaking to me as if *they* have discovered the idea of sharing knowledge as an organizational strategy and that *I'm* the one holding back progress.

The Zambia story finally gave Denning the breakthrough he needed. It helped the World Bank executives envision a different kind of future for their organization. And so they embraced the idea. It became their own. For a few months, there were smaller battles to be won. But the disagreements never lasted long. And by October 1, 6 months after the meeting, president of the World Bank Jim Wolfensohn announced knowledge management was to be a strategy cornerstone. And it's remained so ever since.

■ ■ ■

Stories seem to have the ability to engage people, to make them *care* about the message. When Denning became responsible for knowledge management at the World Bank, the topic wasn't a priority. It wasn't a subject people cared about. He tried to reach out to their minds and tell them otherwise. But that didn't get him very far. As a last resort, he tried something different. He reached out with a story. It worked.

But why did the story work while his arguments didn't? Because his Zambia story got his audience involved:

> If listeners are stimulated to think actively about the implications [of an idea], they can understand what it will be like to be doing things in a different way. When a story does its job, the listeners' minds race ahead to imagine the further implications of elaborating the same idea in other contexts, more intimately known to them.

Denning's experience shows us that stories, besides improving the stickiness of an idea, provide a second benefit. Stories engage. And while listeners are engaged, they're able to imagine new idea perspectives with minimal guidance. Stories tend to put our brains into a different mode, one different to the 'critic mode' when we rationally evaluate the information we receive. As narrative expert David Hurchens points out, "Stories puts listeners in a different orientation. When people hear a good story, they put their pens and pencils down, open up their posture, and just listen." Stories bypass our critic mode. They go straight for the heart.

3.
The Heart of Change

With the help of Deloitte Consulting, John Kotter and Dan Cohen interviewed 400 people from 130 organizations around the world. Their goal... to find out how change happens in organizations. The surprising results are presented in *The Heart of Change*:

> Our main finding, put simply, is that the central issue is never strategy, structure, culture, or systems. All those elements— and others—are important. But the core of the matter is always about changing behavior of people and behavioral change happens in highly successful situations mostly by speaking to people's feelings. ... In highly successful change efforts, people find ways to help others see the problems or solutions in ways that influence emotions, not just thought. ... Conversely, in less successful cases, this seeing-feeling-changing pattern is found less often, if at all.

In other words, it's an emotional connection that kick-starts travelers, not the rationality of the idea itself. This comes as a surprise. Most of us go for a 'Head' approach to convince others about our great idea. We look for best practices, compile a few well-selected graphs, list all the benefits, and arrange our findings in a smart PowerPoint presentation.

But Kotter and Cohen point out that a rational framework—the Head connection—is only effective on its own when "Parameters are known, assumptions are minimal, and the future isn't fuzzy." For example, when you have to decide on a different route to work or to buy a gift for a friend. When most parameters are unknown and the future is blurred—words that wonderfully summarize a strategy journey— the rational approach alone doesn't work. Why? Because of the level of uncertainty the unknown, new situation brings. And rational arguments don't help to overcome that reluctance to change.

Kotter and Cohen's research reveals that the sequence of change in successful change efforts isn't *analyze-think-change,* but rather *see-feel-change.* They found that by showing people a problem and potential solution in a very concrete and compelling way, it reduces negative emotions that block execution. Think about feelings like complacency, pessimism, confusion, and panic. It also increases positive emotions that help adopt the idea. Think about feelings like passion, faith, trust, urgency, hope, and pride.

Denning went for the heart when he saw that his rational approach alone didn't work. With the Zambia story, he made the executives *see* the possibilities of knowledge management (*see what knowledge management can do for people, imagine if we were providing this kind of knowledge, think what an organization we could become!*)

Remember Donald Berwick and his campaign to save 100,000 lives? Berwick knew there would be a lot of resistance to change. It's one thing to know there are a lot of people dying of wrongdoings in hospitals, but it's another to admit it's happening in *your* hospital. If he wanted hospitals to adopt the 6 tactics to prevent wrongful deaths, he first had to get them to admit their hospital wasn't perfect. He knew statistics wouldn't help. Everyone already knew them *(remember the landmark report from the US Institute of Medicine?)*. To succeed, he had to reach out to their hearts. He had to make them *feel* different. How? He had to reduce their negative emotions *(Complacency: there's nothing we can do about it, Fear: we'll get tons of lawsuits if we admit something, Panic: I will lose my job if they find out)*, and strengthen the positive ones *(Pride: I'm proud to be part of a campaign that will save 100,000 lives, Faith: this time we'll be able to make a difference)*.

One of the things Berwick did was to ask Sorrel King to the stage. King told a gripping story about the death of her baby daughter Josie who had died from severe dehydration and misused narcotics. Two careless human errors. But King's story wasn't a bitter one. Her story did clearly deliver the message of hospital error, but it also carried a large measure of hope for the future. Here's how King ended her story:

> On top of our overwhelming sorrow and intense grief, we were consumed by anger. They say anger can do one of two things to you. It can cause you to rot away or it can propel you forward. There were days when all I wanted was to destroy the hospital and then put an end to my own pain. My 3 remaining children were my only reason for getting out of bed and functioning. One day, I will tell them how they saved my life. My husband Tony and I decided that we had to let the anger move us forward. We would do something good that would help prevent this from ever happening to a child again.

4.
A Strategy Wrapper

Kotter and Cohen teach us an important lesson. Often, we believe others will be motivated to help us get our great idea to the finish line. If only we can make them *understand* our idea. But people are reluctant to change when there's a lot of uncertainty. *(Which is always the case on a strategy journey, isn't it?).* To overcome this inertia, we need to make travelers *care* about our idea before anything else. It's the emotional connection that kick-starts travelers. Successful strategists aim for the heart first.

Stories are excellent emotional conductors. Stories, unlike Power-Point presentations or Excel spreadsheets, have the ability to trigger an emotional reaction and facilitate Heart connections. The power of storytelling isn't new. It has been known for thousands of years. And it's served many cultures. Australia's Aborigines use stories as a prop to pass along important messages about the land and their culture. The Sto:lo community in Canada focus on reinforcing their children's identity by telling stories about the land to describe their roles. Politicians aren't afraid of using a little drama and storytelling to get their message across either. And marketers are, above anything, storytellers—as marketing guru Seth Godin points out.

Strategists too can benefit from the power of storytelling. Stories can help us increase message stickiness and involve travelers emotionally with our ideas.

Let's return to Lisa's Mailbox Dilemma and give it a try. Remember the choice she faced? Efficiency versus customer satisfaction. We were able to help her by providing a List of Noes and additional prioritization information. But Lisa's isn't the only mail carrier in the company. She has 8,000 colleagues, probably all struggling with the same strategy trade-off. To help them, let's see if we can wrap a story around her experience:

Lisa Parker, a mail carrier from the Chicago area, struggled with her daily round. She wanted to finish it in time, but she also wanted to engage with her clients. And that required time. As she didn't know how to solve the issue, she brought up the issue at a team meeting. To her surprise, most of her colleagues were struggling with the same issue.

With the help of team leader Eric Reed, they came up with a program called '3 times, 5 a day.' The idea was very simple. They knew they couldn't stop and talk to everyone. But they also knew that the number of clients they'd run into on an average day was pretty limited as most people were at work. So their goal was to talk with 3 clients for 5 minutes a day. This meant they could finish the mail route within the agreed timeframe *and* engage with their clients.

A pilot group of 10 mail carriers, including Lisa, took part in a 90-minute training program on how to start, conduct, and end a 5-minute client conversation.

The concept was simple, but brilliant. Soon after its launch, it became a sport to spot customers. One mail carrier said, "It's like bird watching. Some clients you see every day, but others seem to hide and you have to track them down. Those are the ones that give real satisfaction." They would keep scores using house numbers for each client they spoke to, trying to meet each person behind each door at least once. Some proactively rang the doorbells and introduced themselves. And when someone was finally able to talk to a 'rare' client, their colleagues applauded them at the end of the day. "It really helped us to boost client satisfaction within the efficiency constraints we have," Lisa said enthusiastically.

Did you notice that the core message is the same? Efficiency still comes first. The only difference is the decision context. I've wrapped a story around the core idea, one that fits the context of a mail carrier. And by doing this, I achieve 2 things. First, I improve the stickiness of the idea *(it's easier to remember the core message with such a story, it's also more fun to share)*. Secondly, I give the idea an emotional charge to facilitate the Heart connection *(Faith: this doesn't look so hard. I can do this too. Pride: see what my colleagues did. Combat complacency: it IS possible to talk to my clients and get back in time. Enthusiasm: I want to be a 'client' watcher as well)*. Now just imagine the executives at Lisa's company using several stories like this one to deliver their core idea to the travelers on the execution road.

5.
Jared Fogle's Story

By now, you might be wondering how strategists create these stories. The answer might surprise you. Strategists don't invent stories. They uncover them—in the same way that a sculptor carves a statue out of solid rock. Stephen Denning didn't invent the Zambia story he used. He heard it in the cafeteria while eating a ham sandwich. And he saw its hidden potential, like a sculptor looking at a solid rock:

> My colleague and I were swapping stories and discussing the idea of knowledge sharing. He told me about something that happened to him recently. He has been traveling in Africa—in Zambia, a country about the size of France, but with only a fifth of the population and very low incomes—where he was working on an investment project aimed at improving health services to families, particularly mothers and children. He comes across a health worker in Kamana, a small town some 375 miles from the capital Lusaka. The health worker was trying to find the solution to a problem in treating malaria. At the time, the Zambia story was just a fascinating anecdote. But later, I realized that the example could be incorporated into my arsenal of arguments. It

showed that the idea of sharing know-how isn't completely abstract and hypothetical.

So a strategist isn't a novelist, but rather a diligent story collector. "As I see it," says Tom Peters in his book *Leadership,* "An effective leader, as she makes her rounds at her organization, must ask one—and only one—question: 'Got any good stories?'" Chip and Dan Heath, who we met earlier, illustrate the process of story discovery with a beautiful story about Jared, an obese college student who started eating junk food to lose weight.

In the late 90's, Jared Fogle was severely overweight. We're talking 425 pounds, XXXXXXL shirts, and pants with a 60-inch waist. Jared's father, a general practitioner in Indianapolis, had been warning him about his weight for years. But to little effect. It wasn't until his roommate, a pre-med major, spotted his swollen ankles and correctly diagnosed edema—a dangerous condition that causes diabetes and heart problems, Jared got the wake-up call he needed.

By spring break, Jared had decided to lose weight and get healthy. He'd seen Subway's ad campaign '7 Under 6' *(7 subs under 6 grams of fat)* promoting its healthy range of sandwiches. He took a trip to his nearest Subway. He tasted his first turkey club and liked it. That day, Jared decided to start his own all-Subway diet—a foot-long veggie sub for lunch and a 6-inch turkey sub for dinner. It happened to be a decision that would change his life.

For 3 months, Jared rigidly stuck to his 'Subway Diet', as he called it. In that short period, Jared lost almost 100 pounds. He decided to carry on with it and, as soon as he was physically able, started walking everywhere.

One day, he bumped into Ryan Coleman, his former dorm mate. Coleman was astonished at his transformation. Inspired, he wrote an article for the *Indiana Daily Student* describing what life had been like for the obese Jared. The article concluded with Jared crediting Subway's contribution to his achievement, "Subway helped save my life and start over. I can't ever repay that."

Fast-food chains are rarely credited with transforming someone's health for the better. The story was picked up by a *Men's Health* reporter who was putting together an article on 'Crazy Diets That Work'. Without going into too much detail or even including Jared's name, he mentioned the 'Subway sandwich diet' and 'Subway sandwiches' in general.

But the mention was enough to be spotted by Subway franchise owner Bob Ocwieja. He instantly saw advertising potential in the story. As chairman of the local advertising trust fund, Ocwieja was due to lunch with their agency, the Chicago office of the Publicis Groupe. They already had an advertising slot booked for January, but listened to Ocwieja's idea anyway.

After the meeting, Publicis' creative director Richard Coad was amused and intrigued by Ocwieja's idea. He decided to follow up on it. So he sent one of their interns to Bloomington, Indiana to track down the mystery 'Subway guy'. The search turned out to be far easier than anticipated. The intern started by visiting the Subway franchise closest to Indiana's University campus. And the counter worker immediately knew that he was talking about Jared.

Victorious and confident that they had uncovered a great story, Coad escalated the idea to his boss Barry Krause, who contacted Subway's marketing director. But the newly appointed executive wasn't enthusiastic. He didn't think the story would work. "Fast foods can't do healthy," he told Krause. And even if they could, there would be a ton of legal issues due to the disclaimers.

But Krause and Coad weren't going to let it go that easily. While Subway wasn't prepared to run the campaign on a national level, some regional Subway franchisees were. But franchisees normally only paid to run the commercials. Who would pay for them to be made? Krause, by now completely convinced of the power of Jared's story, came to the rescue. He decided to make the spots for free.

The first ad ran at the beginning of January 2000, just in time for the onslaught of New Year diet resolutions. The ad showed a photo of Jared in front of his home with his old 60-inch-waist pants and described his Subway diet—including, of course, the obligatory legal disclaimer.

The story was a homerun. Jared became an instant celebrity. The next day, *USA Today* called, as did ABC, and Fox News. And on the third day, so did Oprah Winfrey. Within a few days, Subway's national office called asking if the ad could be adopted for national distribution.

The results? Subway's sales, flat in 1999, made an 18 percent jump in 2000 and another 16 percent leap the year after. Subway still works with Fogle today. A 2008 campaign celebrated a full decade of him maintaining his weight loss. And in 2013, they're celebrating his 15-year milestone. So while Jared is the real hero of the weight-loss story, Ocwieja and Co also deserve credit. They're the ones who saw the story's real potential. They uncovered it.

CHAPTER 7

Climb the Commitment Ladder

There were only 6 people in the conference room. And that was unusual since Peter Wood, executive VP operations, was leading the discussion. But the pressure being put on everyone by the Finance department to finalize budgets was leaving them short of time.

At 9.15am—15 minutes later than scheduled—the monthly project review board meeting began. It was a tough session. There were quite a few deliverables outstanding due to a major delay in the new software. But Peter pushed the team hard and, after 2 hours, they came up with a solid action list to redirect the project issues on the table.

Close to the end, Peter looked at the time and said, "Guys, thanks for your help. I know these are challenging times. But it's crucial for the company's future that we get this project done." A few people around the table nodded. "Do I have your commitment for the action plan?" Peter continued and looked around. Now all 5 people nodded in agreement.

Marion Campbell felt great. She normally did after these review meetings. Projects were her life. She knew that the challenges ahead were tough, but that was all part of the fun. She was eager to do whatever it took to get things done.

Ivan Mitchell was stressed when he walked out of the meeting. Not because it was a bad meeting. On the contrary, he greatly admired Peter's way of handling issues. Nor because of the project. He was a big supporter of the new strategic initiative. No, Ivan was stressed because of the time constraints. If only they'd given him the extra resources he'd requested then things would be simple. He stopped, considered going back to ask for them, but quickly decided against it and carried on his way. He'd been refused twice before. So there was no point in going in for a third rejection. "I'll do my best and see where that takes us," he said to himself. "I'm sure the others are facing similar resource issues. They'll probably get less done than me. Peter can aim his anger at them." Feeling much better, he got into the elevator and pressed the button for the sixth floor.

James Turner was surprised Peter got everyone's agreement on the action points. He was at least expecting some resistance. He knew that quite a few colleagues didn't support the project. But today they all seemed to agree. "Maybe it's because some of the key players weren't in the meeting," he considered while rushing out of the conference room. James made a mental note to make a few casual calls the following week. He wanted to find out how they *really* felt about the extra work. "If they all stick to their promise, I'll have to free up a few people from the supply chain project to get some of the work done that I've agreed to," he decided. "If not, I'll look bad at the next review board."

Straight after the meeting, Helen Parker checked her phone for messages from Thomas. Since her promotion, she was anxious to please him. And having to go to these stupid project meetings merely to represent her department didn't help. She had to focus on the important parts of her job. "Meeting with new vendor in Room 15.03. Need you there ASAP," she read. While running to the elevator, cursing her lateness, the action plan evaporated from her mind.

Daniel Cox, one of the veterans of the organization, hovered around the conference room. He tried to get hold of Helen and James, knowing that they weren't huge fans of the project either. He knew he'd have to settle with voicing his frustrations to them as Mark and Debra—the 2 strongest project opponents—weren't in the meeting. But he was out of luck. They seemed to have other things on their minds. James was already on his way out and Helen fumbled nervously with her phone. But his luck changed while he was walking back to his office. He ran into Debra. They both went for a coffee and a smoke. He told her that she'd made the right choice not to go and rambled on about Peter and his stupid project. They should *all* stay away next time. That would teach him a lesson.

A month later, right after the next review meeting, Peter felt completely drained. The project was still way behind schedule. "What went wrong?" he contemplated. "Everyone agreed with the action plan last time." He was still brooding on it when he walked into his fourth meeting of the day.

1.
The Micro-commitment Ladder

The Merriam-Webster Dictionary defines "being engaged" as "greatly interested, committed." The simplest expression of human engagement is the word *yes*. The simplest expression of disengagement is the word *no*. 'Yes' means, "I'm engaged and I'll do it." 'No' means, "I'm not engaged and I won't do it." Yes and no are the engagement core, the molecules of the commitment atom.

But even at the micro-level, engagement doesn't work as dictionaries define it. *Most of the yeses we get are noes in disguise.* By studying the yeses that go back and fore between individuals, I've discovered that you can categorize them into 5 levels. Together, the 5 yeses form *the Micro-commitment Ladder.* To understand the different rungs of the ladder, let's take a closer look at Peter's story. As you've seen, 5 people said 'yes' to him. But as you've probably realized, only the first yes—that of Marion—reflects true execution engagement. The others range from a vague commitment to an actual execution boycott.

The highest rung on the Micro-commitment Ladder is Marion's *Big Yes.* It means, "Yes, I will get it done no matter what." This is the yes we want. And it's the yes we should give to others. *(It's also the yes most people think they got when they hear the word 'yes').* When someone gives us a Big Yes, we have confirmation that this person has taken full ownership of the task at hand. Execution responsibility has truly shifted.

The second rung on the Micro-commitment Ladder is Ivan's *If I Have Time Yes.* This is the, "Yes, I'd like to contribute to the idea, but I have so many other things to do that I'm not sure I'll be able to get it all done in time." When we get this yes, we get an effort commitment. The individual promises to give it a shot when time allows. The task will probably get done to some extent, but we don't get any guarantees. It's not clear if the execution responsibility shifted.

Next in line is James' *Political Yes.* This is the *"*Yes, I might do what's on my action list but only if there's no other way of avoiding it." The person delivering a Political Yes isn't willing to stick his neck out. He will only commit when he sees that others are committed as well. He only moves out of self-interest.

The fourth rung on the Micro-commitment Ladder is Helen's *Coward's Yes.* This affirmation really means, "Yes, I will say 'yes', but only because I'm afraid to lose my... *(position, influence... add as appropriate).*" This person doesn't buy into the idea at all but is afraid of the consequences of being honest. The Coward's Yes is the easy way out of a no. It's used a lot when individuals have no intention of getting much of the work done, but want to postpone the issue until the deliverables are due.

The fifth and lowest rung on the Micro-commitment Ladder is Daniel's *Guerrilla Yes*. He produced a 'yes' during the meeting only because he believed it to be a smarter tactic to fight the battle elsewhere. He really meant, "I don't like the idea and I will do my best to undermine the overall goal by voicing my 'no' privately to others in the hope that a mutiny will force you to abort your goal." People delivering a Guerilla Yes are against our idea. And they will try everything in their power to sabotage its journey to success.

■ ■ ■

Like Peter, we often believe that people are committed to our idea because we got a yes. But reality shows a different picture. Just because someone said 'yes' to our idea doesn't mean something is going to happen. Most of the yeses we get are noes in disguise.

A few years ago, I did a little experiment to quantify the problem. I asked 50 business people to count the number of times they said 'yes' at work on a single day. It turned out to be between 25 and 40 times, with an average of 35. Next, I asked the same individuals anonymously to categorize their yeses, using the 5 steps on the Micro-commitment Ladder. The results were mind blowing. Only 28 percent of the yeses were categorized as Big Yeses. Now, imagine you work for a company of 1,000 people. That's 22,750 expressions of non-commitment packaged as a 'yes' on a single day!

To increase overall strategy engagement, strategists need to find a way to increase micro-commitment. We should go after big commitments on small things. We have several tactics to do this. The first one is straightforward. We should challenge every yes we get and give. In practice, it means we only deliver real commitments ourselves and challenge others to do the same. This doesn't require special skills, only the right mindset. The second tactic is more challenging. We want to offer team members an alternative to express non-commitment. We want to make the word 'no' an acceptable alternative to the fake yeses.

2.
Make NO Acceptable

When an 86-year-old man was brought into Rhode Island's emergency room after falling at home, a scan revealed that he had suffered a subdural hematoma. In other words, blood was pooling in the left side of his head, putting pressure against the tissue in his skull. If the blood wasn't drained quickly, he would die.

The neurosurgeon, who was in the middle of a routine operation, was paged. He stepped away from the operating table to look at the images of the man's head and told the nurse to organize for his wife to sign the consent form. *(Before any surgical procedure, a patient or family member signs a document approving each procedure and verifying the details).*

The patient was brought into the operating theater. A nurse looked at the patient's medical chart and consent form. Leafing through the paperwork, he told the surgeon that there was nothing in the forms about which side of the man's head the hematoma was.

"I saw the scans before," the surgeon said. "It was the right side of the head. If we don't do this quickly, he's going to die."

"Maybe we should pull up the films again?" the nurse suggested and moved towards the computer, which had locked out after being left idle.

"We don't have time," repeated the surgeon, "They told me he's crashing."

"What if we find the family?" the nurse hinted.

"If that's what you want, call the fucking ER and find the family! In the meantime, I'm going to save his life," snapped the surgeon. He grabbed the paperwork, scribbling 'right' next to his initials on the consent form.

"There," he said. "We have to operate immediately."

Having been at the hospital for a year, the nurse knew how it worked. He'd also seen the surgeon's name scribbled in black on the whiteboard—a warning sign to all nursing staff that you shouldn't contradict him… or there'd be trouble. So the nurse put down the chart and stood to one side as the doctor opened up the right side of the man's skull, only to discover that there was no hematoma. *He was operating on the wrong side of the head.* They turned the man quickly, drilled into the other side of his head, found the hematoma, and drained the blood. But the operation had taken almost twice as long. The man was taken into intensive care. He died two weeks later.

The family argued that the trauma of the medical error had overwhelmed him. That if it wasn't for the mistake, he might still be alive. The hospital paid a settlement and the surgeon was barred from ever working at Rhode Island Hospital again.

■ ■ ■

Mahatma Ghandi once said, "A no uttered from the deepest conviction is better than a yes merely uttered to please, or worse, to avoid trouble." But, let's be frank, in most organizations the word 'no' is a dirty word—an unacceptable expression used only by the lazy, unloyal ones.

At Rhode Island Hospital, there were doctors who didn't accept 'no'. And nurses did what they could to avoid expressing it. They developed a color-coded system where writing doctors' names on whiteboards was a way of warning each other. Blue meant 'nice', red meant 'jerk', and black 'don't contradict them or you're in trouble.' The doctor who made the fatal mistake was labeled black.

In an environment where 'no' is unacceptable, people don't dare to challenge decisions. In such an environment, individuals are more afraid of the consequences of disagreeing than the consequences of someone's wrong decision. Even if lives are at stake. Take a look at the following cockpit conversation between the first officer and captain on a cold winter's day in January, shortly before take-off:

First officer: "Look how the ice is just hanging on his, ah, back there, see that?"

(*waits*)

First officer: "See all those icicles on the back there and everything?"

(*waits*)

First officer: "Boy, this is a, this is a losing battle here on trying to de-ice those things, it [gives] you a false feeling of security, that's all that it does."

Shortly after being given clearance to take off, the first officer expresses his concern for the fourth time.

First officer: "Let's check those [wing] tops again since we've been sitting here a while."

Captain: "I think we get to go here in a minute."

Finally, when they were on their take-off roll, the first officer noticed that something was wrong with the engine readings.

First officer: "That don't seem right, does it?" (3 seconds pause). "Ah, that's not right."

Captain: "Yes, it is, there's 80."

First officer: "Naw, I don't think that's right." (7 second pause). "Ah, maybe it is."

Minutes later, the Air Florida aircraft failed to gain sufficient height on take-off. It crashed into the nearby Potomac River. There were only 5 survivors.

3.
Mitigated Speech

Unfortunately, the co-pilot's inability to trigger the right decision from the pilot isn't a tragic stand-alone fact. According to US National Transportation Safety Board (NTSB) research, this type of communication failure occurred in 75 percent of all plane accidents.

In a potentially life-threatening situation such as the Air Florida cockpit or Rhode Island Hospital, we would expect subordinates to be very explicit in their communication. We would expect the nurse to say, "Don't do anything until we get confirmation," and the first officer, "Don't take off until we've checked our wings again." Instead, they only hinted. The communication phenomenon that explains why subordinates downplay the meaning of their message when addressing their boss is called *Mitigated Speech*. It's villain number 5 on the execution road.

To understand his mode of operation, it's important to realize that communication isn't just a matter of *transferring information,* like the nurse pointing out that facts are missing on the chart or the co-pilot saying that de-icing is a losing battle. Often, the speaker also wants to *influence the behavior* of the listener. In our examples, the nurse wanted the doctor to have confirmation *before* deciding which side of the old man's skull to drill. And the co-pilot wanted the captain to check for ice again *before* deciding to take off.

Instead of clearly suggesting the required action, subordinates tend to downplay their decision advice. Why? Because of *social considerations*. Research shows that the status of both the speaker and listener influence the directness of their speech. If you're the boss, you can command others to do something. That comes with the job. But if you're a subordinate using the same command, you may be seen as threatening or rude. To avoid this kind of confrontation, subordinates are likely to use more polite and indirect ways of communicating. They tend to soften the message. They mitigate.

Researchers Ute Fischer and Judith Orasanu gave a group of captains and first officers the following hypothetical scenario:

> While cruising, you notice on the weather radar an area of heavy precipitation 25 miles ahead. First officer Henry Jones, who is flying the aircraft, is maintaining his present course at Mach .73 even though embedded thunderstorms have been reported in your area and you encounter moderate turbulence. You want to ensure that your aircraft does not penetrate this area.
> They then asked, "What would you say to Jones?"

Fischer and Orasanu believed there were at least 6 different ways of persuading the captain to change course, each with a different level of mitigation:

1. Command: "Turn 30 degrees right." This is the most direct form of communication. There's no doubt on the action requested. No mitigation here.
2. Crew Obligation Statement: "We need to deviate right about now." This statement is a bit softer. Notice the 'we' format. It's stated as a joined decision.
3. Crew suggestion: "Let's go around the weather."

4.   Query: "Which direction would you like to deviate?"
5.   Preference: "I think it would be wise to turn left or right."
6.   Hint: "That return at 25 miles looks mean." This statement
      is the most mitigated. Notice that there isn't a suggestion
      anymore. The social compliance to hierarchy took over.

The results? While most captains reported that they would issue the
command, "Turn 30 degrees right," most of the first officers chose the
hint. At Rhode Island Hospital, we saw the nurse use the same type
of vague statements, saying things like "Maybe we should pull up
the films again?" and, "What if we find the family?" His interventions
showed that he clearly felt uncomfortable with the doctor's next decision. He feared the surgeon would choose the wrong side of the brain.
But his fear of challenging the doctor's decision—someone higher up
the hospital's hierarchy and labeled by colleagues as someone who
doesn't accept 'no'—was even greater. And so he only delivered a few
weak hints which had absolutely no impact on changing the surgeon's
course of action.

■ ■ ■

Fisher and Orasanu also wanted to know which of the 6 communication options was the most effective to correct decision errors. In other
words, when we feel someone is going to make the wrong decision,
what's the most effective way to stop them? To find the answer, they
provided 59 captains and 57 first officers from 3 major US airlines the
incident description from the first experiment and an example of each
of the options. Participating captains were told that the communica-
tions were from first officers. First officers received the same communication and were told that they were from captains. Participants from
both groups were then asked to rate how effective each communica-

tion would be in getting them to carry out the speaker's intent—to change the course of the airplane—while maintaining a positive crew environment.

While striking differences were found in the captains' and first officers' communication methods—as the first experiment illustrated—there was considerable agreement on what constituted effective communication. Both groups selected Crew Obligation Statements (option 2) and Preference Statements (option 3) as the most effective. In other words, both groups agreed on what effective communication in the cockpit should be like, but neither pilots nor first officers took advantage of this knowledge when they were actually *in* a cockpit.

4.
Crew Resource Management

Once the aviation industry understood the primary cause of aviation accidents to be human error, fighting the villain Mitigated Speech in the cockpit became a priority. Their combat strategy? *Crew Resource Management.*

CRM empowers individuals to challenge decisions effectively. Everybody in the team is encouraged to think and debate together. The methodology is based on the observed traits of successful crews, like sharing opinions openly, looking at evidence from different angles, and considering alternatives instead of ignoring them.

Multiple studies show the benefits of CRM. One assessment showed a 91 percent flight performance improvement, while another inquiry indicated 85 percent. And, most importantly, accidents related to wrong decisions drastically decreased. Take Korean Air. Once an airline with one of the highest accident rates, it turned itself around by adopting Crew Resource Management. Today, the airline is a proud member of Star Alliance and one of the safest in the world. A few years ago, it was given the Phoenix Award by *Air Transport World* in recognition of its incredible transformation.

Once the success stories from the cockpit started to spread, the healthcare industry—which had similar communication problems in its operating rooms—got interested. They adopted CRM. Nurses were encouraged to express their opinions to doctors. And everyone got involved in post-mortem debriefings to evaluate decision making. Numerous studies demonstrated equally impressive figures in the battle against Mitigated Speech—from a drastic 58 percent reduction of observable errors and a 19 percent improvement in team satisfaction to serious cost savings by reducing the average length of stay in the emergency department.

When another 'accident' happened, Rhode Island Hospital decided to use the crisis as a turnaround. They invested heavily in education and taught staff how to express a clear 'no' using the crew concept of the airline industry. Their efforts paid off. Today, Rhode Island Hospital is one of the leading hospitals in the US. Since they've adopted the new approach, no wrong-site errors have occurred. The hospital also received honors from the American College of Surgeons for the quality of its cancer care. And it earned a Beacon Award, the most prestigious recognition for critical care nursing. Rhode Island Hospital had beaten the villain.

■ ■ ■

Crew Resource Management improves decision making. The CRM results in cockpits and operating rooms teach us that co-pilots and nurses can effectively challenge decisions. They can express a clear no and suggest an alternative path. They just need to learn how.

And that's great news for us. *We can improve decision making on our strategy journey too by teaching travelers how to challenge deci-sions effectively.* Successful strategists help create an environment where social considerations don't block effective communication. They offer team members a universal, acceptable way to show their non-commitment. They provide a framework to challenge decisions and offer alternatives, all while keeping the team spirit high.

And when 'no' becomes an acceptable word to express non-com-mitment—an alternative to the fake yeses on the Micro-commitment Ladder—the overall decision quality improves. And wonderful things can happen, just like in the intensive care unit of this hospital.

A seriously ill, newborn baby was lying in a neonatal intensive-care unit, carefully monitored by the nurse on duty. She was especially vigi-lant as his color was varying from a normal healthy pink to a worrying gray color *(color being a good indication of potential problems).*

Suddenly, the baby's color changed again. But this time, he turned almost black. The intensive care team jumped into action calling for a doctor and X-ray technician. They believed that the tiny baby had suf-fered a collapsed lung *(a common problem for babies on ventilators)* and quickly prepared themselves, getting ready to pierce the baby's chest and insert a tube in order to suck out the air from around the lung to allow it to re-inflate.

But the watching nurse had seen this ominous blue-black color before. This wasn't a collapsed lung, she thought. This was a pneu-mopericardium—a heart problem—where air fills the sac around the heart, placing enough pressure on it to stop it beating. And she was filled with terror because last time she'd seen it, the baby had died be-fore they found out.

She had to stop them. But in response to her cries, "It's the heart!" and her desperate pleas to stop their preparations to treat the lung, they simply pointed at the heart monitor. One hundred and thirty beats per minute. A perfectly normal heart rate for a newborn.

But the nurse refused to back down. She had to find a way to change their course of action. After pushing them away and screaming for quiet, she checked for a heartbeat. And just as she expected, there wasn't one.

As she started compressions, the chief neonatologist appeared. "Stick the heart," the nurse insisted, "it's a pneumopericardium." With her diagnosis confirmed by a scan, the neonatologist guided the syringe into the boy's heart instantly releasing the air that was suffocating it. The heart started beating. The baby's color returned. His life was saved.

Only when the nurse had tried to listen to the heart with the stethoscope had it become clear that the heart had actually stopped. The air in the sac around the heart had prevented it from beating, despite the fact that the heart nerves were still firing. But since heart monitors measure electrical activity rather than heartbeats, the heart rate seemed perfectly normal to all of those in the room... except for one. The nurse had saved the young baby's life.

CHAPTER 8

Go Beyond Self-interest

When Roger Bannister finished fourth in the 1500-meter final at the 1952 Olympics, he was disappointed. So disappointed that he considered giving up running. Luckily he didn't. Instead, he set himself a new goal. A goal that was even more challenging than winning a medal at the Olympics. He then intensified his training schedule and got to work.

Two years later, Bannister was set to race at the Iffley Road Track in Oxford. With winds of up to 25 miles per hour prior to the race, he had originally decided not to run. He wanted to save his energy and make the attempt at another meet. But when the wind dropped shortly before the race, Bannister decided to go for it, with Chris Chataway and Chris Brasher as pacemakers. Three thousand spectators watched the 6 runners. Bannister and Brasher went immediately into the lead. After the second lap, Chataway took over and moved into the lead. He continued around the front turn until Bannister began his finishing kick with half a lap to go. Once over the finish line, the crowd waited anxiously for stadium announcer Norris McWhirter to confirm the time, "Ladies and gentlemen, here's the result of event 9, the one mile: 1st, No. 41, R.G. Bannister, Amateur Athletic Association and former- ly of Exeter and Merton Colleges, Oxford, with a time which is a new meeting and track record, and which—subject to ratification—will be a new English Native, British National, All-Comers, European, British Empire and World Record. The time was 3..."

On hearing the number '3', the roar of the crowd drowned out the end of his sentence. Bannister's final time was 3 minutes, 59.4 seconds.

For years, it had been considered humanly impossible, even physi- cally dangerous, to run a mile in under 4 minutes. But on May 6 1954, 2 years after his defeat at the Olympics, Bannister did the impossible. He ran a sub-4-minute mile. His achievement was so significant that Forbes named it one of the greatest athletics achievements of all time. Bannister's legacy continues today. In 2012, he carried the Olympic flame in the stadium named after him.

But the bizarre part of the story is yet to come. Within 3 years of Banister's 'impossible' achievement, 16 other athletes did the same. They *all* ran a sub-4-minute mile.

1.
Bandura's Theory

So how come that running a mile in less than 4 minutes had proved impossible for decades? Then one individual—Roger Bannister—does the impossible and, within 3 years, 16 others do the same? The simple answer: belief. When Bannister smashed the elusive 4-minute mile, he also destroyed a psychological barrier. His performance turned the default setting in people's heads from 'impossible' to 'possible'. Other runners saw the finish line within their grasp. Non-belief didn't hold them back anymore. The more elaborate answer to the most amazing sport event of the 20th century requires us to understand the particular human dynamics that make people believe.

Although everyone can pick a goal, few are able to carry through and achieve success. Just think about those 88 percent of individuals who don't follow through on their New Year's resolutions. Albert Bandura, one of the most influential psychologists of the last 50 years, found a key to increasing the success rate. He found that an individual's self-efficacy—*the belief in one's capabilities to get things done*—plays a major role in the success or failure of goals.

Bandura's Theory states that individuals who believe in their own success share 4 characteristics: (1) They view challenging problems as tasks to be mastered; (2) They develop a deeper interest in activities in which they participate; (3) They form a stronger sense of commitment to their interests and activities; and (4) They recover faster from setbacks and disappointments.

It's not hard to imagine Roger Bannister as having a phenomenal belief in his own abilities. He bounced back right after being defeated at the Olympics *(characteristic 4)*. He approached the sub-4-minute-mile—a challenge that no one else considered feasible—as a task, breaking down the overall 'impossible' goal into smaller pieces, each seemingly more feasible *(characteristic 1)*. He tried and tested innovative training practices with a scientific passion *(characteristic 2)*. And if you consider these 3 factors and include his grueling training schedule, it's fair to say that it would've been hard to find anyone more committed to running a sub-4-minute mile than Roger Bannister *(characteristic 3)*.

Bannister believed he could succeed. And his belief triggered his body and mind to draw on the resources to do so. He didn't deliberately sit down and decide to give greater commitment to the goal, or to recover faster from his Olympic setback. This all happened automatically when he started to believe. Bannister became the first human to run the sub-4-minute mile because *he truly believed he could.*

■ ■ ■

Bandura's Theory states that our performance gets a boost if we believe in success. Belief triggers a set of human processes that facilitate goal achievement. Belief makes us dig deeper, get up quicker, and keep going longer. And by doing so, we drastically increase our chances of reaching the finish line.

The way we see ourselves perform and the belief we have in our qualifications to do so, are shaped in early childhood. As children, we deal with a wide variety of experiences, tasks, and situations. It's the basis for how we look at ourselves. But our self-efficacy growth doesn't have to end when we turn 18. As we can acquire new skills, experiences, and understanding, we can also grow our belief in our abilities. *We can grow our self-confidence.* And that's great news. It means we can all tap into the benefits of believing. According to Bandura's Theory, there are 4 major sources we can draw from:

1. Past Successes: *"I've done it before, so I can do it again"*
2. Modeling: *"If he can do it, I can do it as well"*
3. Verbal Persuasion: *"You can do it!"*
4. Emotional Arousal: *"The discomforts I feel are just discomforts"*

Out of these 4, the first is the strongest. Our past successes have the biggest impact on our belief system. Performing a task successfully strengthens our sense of self-efficacy. *Past successes make us believe we can be successful again in the future.* Bannister tapped into his past successes to increase belief. On May 2 1953, he made an attempt on the British record at Oxford. Paced by Chris Chataway, Bannister ran 4:03.6, shattering Wooderson's 1945 standard. "This race made me realise that the 4-minute mile was not out of reach," Bannister said afterwards. He also fueled his belief by successfully mastering the sub-tasks he defined. He successfully ran 7 straight half-miles at an average time of 2:03, 10 straight quarter-miles at an average of 58.9, three-quarters of a mile in 2:59.8, and a half-mile in 1:54.

Witnessing other people succeed is the second most important source to boost self-belief. Bandura points out that, "Seeing people similar to oneself succeed by sustained effort raises observers' beliefs that they too possess the capabilities to master comparable activities required to succeed." In other words, *if he can do it, I can do it as well.* Clearly, modeling helps explain why those 16 runners were able to run a sub-4-minute mile *after* Bannister succeeded rather than *before.* Bannister's success triggered their belief system. His race was a cue that said, "If Bannister can do it, I can do it." And their new-found belief made them draw on resources they didn't tap into before. Up to that point, they didn't have a role model. After Bannister's magic race, they did. And it made them run faster than ever before.

A third dynamic that fuels belief is verbal persuasion. People are susceptible to the opinions of others. We can be persuaded to believe. Just think about an occasion when a friend encouraged you. Getting verbal encouragement from others helps us to overcome self-doubt, giving our best effort to the task at hand. Verbal persuasion, however, is a double-edged sword. *Positive words increase belief, negative ones reduce it.* And it proves that discouragement is generally more effective at decreasing a person's self-efficacy than encouragement is at increasing it. Before Bannister's historic race, everyone said that running a sub-4-minute mile wasn't possible. These negative comments found its way into the heads of those 16 runners. They were verbally modeled in a negative way. It was like everyone saying to them, "You can't do it."

The fourth and final source we can draw from to boost our belief in success, is our ability to deal with our emotional response to stressful situations. Stress-related moods and physical reactions can impact a person's feelings about succeeding. 'Butterflies in the stomach' before a crucial race will be interpreted by someone with low self-efficacy as a sign of inability. *I felt uncomfortable before the last race I lost, I feel uncomfortable now, it's clear I will lose again today.* As Bandura points out, it's not the sheer intensity of emotional and physical reactions that is important, but rather how they're perceived and interpreted. By learning how to deal with our emotional arousal in stressful situations, we can improve our belief to succeed. Before the start of Bannister's big race, there was a strong wind. It would have been easy to get caught up, lose concentration, and just give in. He didn't. Bannister knew how to control his nerves. He patiently waited until the last moment before deciding whether or not to run. And when the wind died, he decided to go for it. He crossed the finish line 3 minutes and 59.4 seconds later, clearly unaffected by the weather conditions.

■ ■ ■

What happens if we take Bandura's Theory to the execution road? Strong evidence suggests that the way travelers think about their abilities to succeed has a compelling effect on their motivation, effort, and performance. Travelers who strongly believe in their ability to reach the finish line will outperform those that don't.

We've learned that we can influence belief. By highlighting the past accomplishments of individuals, we give them a boost, just like Bannister drew strength from his British record and past successes on shorter distances. *You've done it before, you can do it again. The finish line isn't a far-off dream, but a destination within reach.* By sharing success stories of others, we provide role models, just like Bannister became a role model for those 16 runners. *If he can do it, you can do it as well.* And by creating a positive environment where successes are verbally reinforced and psychological hardships downplayed, we cultivate a 'can do' spirit in the team. *Embrace your challenges. You have what it takes to succeed. I'm convinced you can do it. You're a winner.*

In a way, *success is a self-fulfilling prophecy.* And the trigger, surprisingly, is belief. When we expect to succeed, we automatically mobilize our internal resources to achieve the expected. All this happens without our rational consent. Mother Nature organizes our victory pursuit. All we need to do is believe in our ability to reach the finish line, just like Roger Bannister did before he ran the race of his life.

2.
The Pygmalion Effect

Dov Eden is a professor at the University of Tel Aviv. He studies belief. And his research reveals a second, probably even more remarkable trait of the impact of belief on performance. Consider a 15-week army course where 105 soldiers were assigned to one of 4 instructors. A few days before the start of the program, each instructor was briefed, including the following message:

> We have compiled much data on the trainees including psychological test scores, sociometric evaluations, grades in previous courses, and ratings by previous commanders. Based on this information, we have predicted the command potential (CP) of each soldier. …Based on CP scores, we have designated each trainee as having either a high, regular or unknown CP, the latter due to incomplete records. When we're not sure, we don't guess. Soldiers of all 3 CP levels have been divided equally among the

4 training classes.

Each instructor was given their list of trainees (one-third of whom had a high CP, one-third a regular CP, and the remainder an unknown CP). They were then asked to copy each trainee's command potential into their personal records and learn the names and scores before they arrived.

It's important to know that, at the time, these 4 instructors didn't know that the command potential classification—the performance score on the list they received—was completely random. In other words, *the soldier listed as having the highest CP could very well be the worst soldier in the group.*

After 16 weeks, at the end of the combat course, the performance of the 105 soldiers was tested in 4 different areas. One of these performance evaluations, for example, was their proficiency in the use of weapons they had been trained to master.

The outcome? Those soldiers who got marked with a high command potential significantly outperformed their classmates in all 4 subjects. Those with an average CP scored the lowest. The third group—those with an unknown performance potential—ended up in the middle. The difference in performance between the best and the worst group was 15 percent.

After detailed analysis, it showed that the experimentally induced expectations—the fake command potential scores—explained almost three-quarters of the variance in performance. In other words, *by making a superior believe a subordinate has the ability to be a great performer, the actual performance increases.* And the effect isn't marginal. It's a whopping 2-digit figure!

Strange, don't you think? When we believe a team member has the ability to be a great performer, our belief becomes reality. The performance expectation we have for our team members is a self-fulfilling prophecy. The scientific name for this phenomenon is *the Pygmalion Effect*. Like Bandura's Theory, it's not a rational 'head' dynamic, but a human 'heart' idiosyncrasy.

■ ■ ■

So what's the secret? How does the Pygmalion Effect work? In short, the Pygmalion Effect is *a leadership phenomenon*. As soon as the instructors believed that some soldiers had better abilities than others, they started managing those individuals differently. "Raising expectations triggers a leadership process that culminates in superior performance," Eden points out. High expectations bring out the best leadership in a manager. *Just imagine those instructors spending more time with 'promising' soldiers, highlighting successes, showing best practices, and teaching them how to deal with stressful situations.* Better leadership, in turn, has a direct, positive effect on the subordinate's performance. It kick-starts the positive effects of Bandura's Theory. *Just imagine the extra boost the belief system from the 'promising' soldiers gets by the extra positive attention from their instructor.*

THE PYGMALION EFFECT

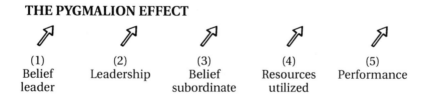

(1)	(2)	(3)	(4)	(5)
Belief leader	Leadership	Belief subordinate	Resources utilized	Performance

But Pygmalion has an evil twin brother called *Golem*. While positive expectations from the leader fuel the self-fulfilling prophecy, negatives ones create a downward spiral that leads to lower performance.

Take the following true story that happened in a factory assembling disposable sterile medical kits for use in blood transfusion. Its plant manager, who had heard a lecture about the Golem Effect, was having a problem with the productivity of new workers. They were either native or Eastern European immigrants. And everyone at the plant 'knew' that the natives were poor workers in comparison to the immigrants. They adjusted slower, took longer to reach standard production, and had difficulty maintaining it. In particular, the head supervisor, who had been responsible for putting new hires to work for years, 'knew' the native women would give her trouble.

The plant manager however believed the native workers to be as capable as the immigrants. As he suspected that the head supervisor had a negative prejudice towards the natives' performance, he told her that he had personally handpicked the native new hires that were to start the following week. He also told her they were excellent people, expected to reach standard production targets quickly. As usual, the head supervisor promised to report any problems to him.

But surprisingly, this time, there weren't any. In fact, it was the smoothest intake of new hires that anyone in the plant could remember. The new native recruits achieved the standard in record time and, soon after, some even outperformed the norm. The supervisor complemented the plant manager for improving his hiring decisions.

Isn't that amazing? Just by raising the expectations in the supervisor's mind, the native group performed outstandingly. The recruits weren't handpicked, but by making the supervisor think they were, her performance expectations of the new recruits changed from negative to positive. Eden argues that when we expect low performance, we get low performance. It's a negative self-fulfilling prophecy—the Golem Effect.

THE GOLEM EFFECT

(1)	(2)	(3)	(4)	(5)
Belief leader	Leadership	Belief subordinate	Resources utilized	Performance

By changing expectations, we can fight this villain. The negative spiral triggered by negative performance expectations *(they can't)* becomes a positive one *(they can)*. The result? Better performance.

A few years ago, I was fortunate to be involved in a project to see both Pygmalion and Golem at work. A large financial institution wanted to fire about 100 employees that had been identified as low performers by their boss. Over a number of years, this group of low performers consistently received a low score on their performance evaluation. According to their superior, they didn't add any value. To comply with the law, senior leadership involved the worker's union. They agreed to the course of action, but challenged the quality of the performance rating. A compromise was found. Over a one-year period, the low performers were individually coached by an independent coach using a positive approach. *They weren't treated as low performers anymore.* At the end of the year, their performance was evaluated again. If it didn't meet company standards, they got fired as initially planned. But if their performance improved, they got to stay and the 'low performer' stigma was definitely removed.

A year later, to the surprise of many, a little over half of the group performed on, or even above standard. When we took a closer look, we found clear evidence that those who relaunched themselves had troubled relationships with their boss. *There was a lack of belief in their ability to succeed, as we saw with the native workers.*

"Leaders get the performance they expect," Eden argues. When we expect low performance, our expectations kick-start a negative spiral that leads to low performance. "Underachievers grow accustomed to getting by with minimally acceptable performance simply because nothing more is expected of them." Just by replacing a management style of negative comments and neglect with a 'can do' approach, it was possible to turn the negative spiral into a positive one for over 50 percent. And this was a group previously identified as chronic low performers. Imagine the power of Pygmalion if we apply a 'can do' management style to *everyone* in the team.

．．．

Both the Pygmalion and Golem Effect are important for us. When we believe our team members have what it takes to succeed on the execution road—like the 4 instructors did with those high CP soldiers—the chance they actually will increases significantly. Higher expectations lead to better performance. But when we expect our fellow travelers to fail—like the supervisor expected from native workers—they probably will.

Eden and Co teach us that we have to be careful in what we believe. Most of us have the habit of labeling team members. Maria is a high performer, Joe is average, Eva reached her ceiling, and Mike is a low performer. *But our labels are self-fulfilling prophecies.* And for those that end up in the high performance category, that's great. They'll get the leader they deserve. But for those that we categorize as average or low performers, it's not. Because when we don't expect greatness, our leadership won't be great either. And by doing so, we contribute to their failure.

If we want to increase strategy success, we have to reconsider the relationship we have with *all* our team members. We need to cultivate a 'can do' environment, a place where we expect success from every team member, not only a few high performers. Army instructors who believe *all* soldiers will succeed have better combat troops than those who don't. Factory supervisors who believe *all* workers will succeed produce more than those who don't. Leaders who believe *all* travelers will succeed outperform those who don't.

IN PART 2 of *The Execution Shortcut*, we've learned a great deal about the travelers on the execution road. On the positive side, travelers have enormous strengths. When they believe, they can do amazing things—more than they've ever imagined—like the 16 runners who replicated Roger Bannister's success. But we've also seen plenty of evidence of the travelers' limitations—their fear to say no, their apathy when they're not engaged, and their indecisiveness when presented with too many options.

Here's the good news: it's possible to tap into the travelers' strengths and circumvent their flaws. Successful strategists who reach out to the hearts of travelers have a triple game plan.

First, they *share strategy stories*. Stories make messages stickier. Wrap a story around your message and it becomes 20 times easier for the listener to remember. Stories stick because they put information in a context that travelers can relate to. Just think about the story we wrapped around Lisa's Dilemma. Stories also offer a second benefit— they facilitate an emotional connection. They reach for the heart. Think about Stephen Denning who got the World Bank to embrace knowledge management against all odds. His Zambia story shifted the executives' mindset from a rational "Do I agree or not with the idea?" to an emotional "Why don't we do this?" And the great thing about stories is that we don't have to invent them. We just have to spot them, like Bob Ocwieja spotted Jared's story, the obese college student who started eating fast food to lose weight.

Next, successful strategists tweak the environment to *boost micro-commitment*. We've learned not to settle for small commitments on big things, but to go for big commitments on small things. We should offer only Big Yeses ourselves and challenge others to do the same. We can help travelers climb the Micro-commitment Ladder by making 'no' an acceptable alternative for the fake yeses. Just think about the amazing success stories in cockpits and emergency rooms. Travelers, just like nurses and co-pilots, can effectively challenge decisions. They just have to learn how.

Finally, successful strategists *boost belief.* We've seen that it's possible to make runners run faster, soldiers fight better, and natives beat immigrants. Surprisingly, the key to success is belief. Bannister ran the race of the century because he believed he could. Sixteen runners ran the race of their lives because they started to believe. A bunch of soldiers outperformed others only because their instructor believed they could. Success is a self-fulfilling prophecy. When we believe, our body and mind gathers resources to dig deeper, recover faster, and keep going longer. When others believe in us, the dynamic is reinforced. Think about the Israeli soldiers. Their instructors' belief made them better soldiers. Like the native workers, they had the ability to succeed. They only needed someone who believed in them so they could believe in themselves.

PART 3

HANDS

CHAPTER 9

Tackle CO$_2$mplexity

I t was a cool evening in the Indian Himalayas. Raju's mind drifted. He was saddened by recent events. And even years of meditation couldn't help him distance himself from his troubled thoughts. Finally, when the sun was long gone, he took a decision and posted his mission on the wall. "So I'll never forget," he said to himself. *His choice would change his life in more ways than he could ever imagine.*

Since Bikash Bandhari, Raju's famous teacher had died 2 months before, almost all Buddhist monks—young and old—had moved away. Some had returned home, others joined a new Zen master in a neighboring monastery. *All except one.* For 2 months, Raju had been contemplating, "Should I finish what I started in my beloved monastery in Toli?"

That night, as soon as he had taken the decision to stay, he felt more relaxed. But Raju knew it wouldn't be easy. He'd need help. "I should find someone who can cook my food and wash my clothes. That would leave me with time to study and meditate."

At first, all went well. But after a few months, the cook got lazy and the maid's mother got sick, forcing her to spent lots of time away from the monastery. Raju ended up hungry and the monastery dirty. He became restless again. "I need a second cook to keep the first one on his toes'" he judged, "and another maid to fill in when the first is off to her mother."

Initially, this new set-up worked well. But after a few months, the 4 servants weren't getting along and Raju was often disturbed to resolve their disputes. *The same dynamic kept repeating itself.* Over the next 3 years, Raju constantly restructured the monastery. It became a full-time job. In the end, he supervised 65 employees, organized regular Kung Fu demonstrations, and ran an on-site guesthouse with a beautiful souvenir shop for visitors. And the words 'Become a Zen master' that were written on the paper fixed on his wall, slowly faded away.

1.
The 100 Things Company

Take a moment to think about your own goal. What would you like to get out of life? What slogan would capture your ambition? And now think about this. How much time did you spend last month working towards that goal? Was it what you hoped for? Was it enough?

Leo Babauta, an overweight, out-of-shape journalist living on the tiny island of Guam, asked himself the same questions. And he honestly answered 'no' to the last 2. He knew only drastic measures would cut him free from a situation that saw him running round in circles like a hamster on a wheel. On February 1 2007, he stared writing about his challenges to get back in shape, even out his work-life balance, and fight his nicotine addiction. Then he became interested in simplicity. He decided to totally embrace it and started The 100 Things

Challenge—a mission to reduce personal possessions to 100 items or fewer. A few years later, Babauta, who now lives in San Francisco, has time to focus on the things he find important. He writes books, travels, walks everywhere (he doesn't own a car anymore), and spends time with his wife and 6 kids. *Cutting complexity worked miracles for him.* On his blog, now one of the 25 most popular in the world, Babauta encourages others to embrace simplicity as well. Now take a moment to think about using the same simplicity concept in your organization. Imagine what it would be like if you could get rid of all the unnecessary complexity. Just think what it would be like to work in a 100 Things Company.

2.
CO$_2$mplexity Kills

Complexity is the CO$_2$ of the modern business world. We've all heard of it, we all produce it, it's harmful to the business environment, and companies tend to ignore it when money's for the making. But unlike CO$_2$, there's no public opinion to point out the dangers. There's no Al Gore on stage. Yes, there are some companies out there with enlightened leaders who have embraced simplification and installed a company culture that fights against the ever-growing complexity. But they're the exception. *Most of us live in a complex business world where simplicity isn't on the agenda.* And according to strategists Chris Zook and James Allen from Bain & Company, that's a big problem. In *Repeatability,* their latest book that summarizes their extensive research to find the Holy Grail of sustained performance, Zook and Allen point out that *complexity is the biggest performance killer in organizations.*

One of the biggest causes for ever-growing complexity in an organization is growth. Growth fuels CO$_2$mplexity in a sneaky way. When companies grow, they become more complex. But CO_2mplexity isn't about that 'one big thing' happening overnight. It's about small things that keep adding up over time—one more KPI here, another survey there, another job created in HQ to manage a new region. Or another management layer to limit the span of control, an extra budget round to challenge the figures from the product lines. And the people inside these companies are like frogs in slowly boiling water; they don't notice the gradual complexity increase. They're so tied up adapting to their changing situation that they don't make any moves to change it. To make it worse, most of us are not only unaware of the ever-growing complexity around us, we're actually part of the problem, adding complexity ourselves. *We're like frogs boiling our own water.*

3.
Size Versus Industry

When you craft a strategy, the industry you compete in highly impacts your choices. Just think about Porter's classic Five Forces' framework. Different entry barriers, rivalry between competitors, substitutes, bargaining power of clients and suppliers, all make an industry unique. Change industry and you have to change strategy.

But does the industry also define the best execution approach? Many leaders believe it does. Eagerly, they examine peer companies and visit conferences to find out about the strategy execution best practices in their field. But their view on the forces that shape good strategy execution doesn't match up with reality. Insights from *the performance factory* suggest that the industry you compete in plays a rather limiting role in selecting the right strategy execution processes and tools. In other words, *it doesn't really matter from which industry your strategy execution best practices come.* A high-quality Balanced

Scorecard approach used in a large telecom company will most probably work just as well in a huge pharmaceutical company. A solid approach to managing the strategic initiatives found in an automotive company will do equally well in a similar sized media company.

There is however a different factor that does have a big impact when it comes to choosing the best execution approach. It's a factor often overlooked by the same leaders. I'm talking about size—or more specifically the size of the group that will be working with the selected execution tools and techniques. Consider the introduction of a Balanced Scorecard (an approach to cascade strategy in the organization). There are several ways to set it up, ranging from an ultra-light, once-a-year, half-day workshop that helps managers reflect on their objectives to a full-blown, permanent process defining, challenging, and monitoring the complete strategy cascade. According to *the performance factory*, the approach you pick—small, medium, or large—should mainly depend on the size of the group that's going to use the scorecard.

One way to make sense of this is to consider group dynamics. Remember the Rule of 150? It suggests that the size of a group can make a big difference. Several studies point out that groups larger than 150 lose their social glue. They then need processes, structures, and tools to compensate. Think about a small business unit of 50 people that needs to define its long-term objectives in line with the corporate strategy. As the boss has direct access to everyone, she will find it quite easy to bring all the information together, discuss assumptions and monitor progress. *She doesn't need a complex framework to cascade strategy.* For a large unit with 1,000 people, it's a totally different story. The boss doesn't have the same access. The social glue is gone. And to compensate, she needs a more structured approach to achieve the same results. When you craft a strategy execution approach, the size of the group that will use your design greatly impacts your choices. *Size is to strategy execution what industry is to strategy.* Change the size of the unit and you have to change the strategy execution approach.

• • •

So what does this mean for us? The fact that size rather than industry drives the choice for the best execution approach has two important consequences for organizing strategy execution process improvements. First of all, rather than limiting our search for best practices in our industry, we should look beyond its borders and search for great examples among companies, business units or teams our size. Our search shouldn't be focused on 'Competitor X (3 times our size) has a great Balanced Scorecard approach. Let's see what we can learn.' It should rather be, 'Company Y, a company our size, has developed a great approach. Let's take a closer look and see what we can learn.'

Secondly, we should scale the chosen solution. Consider you're going on a hiking trip with your family and want to equip everyone with a new backpack. You might consider buying all the same brand because you know it's good quality. But you also want a backpack that's the right size for each person (you don't want a 10-year-old carrying a 35-pound bag). This logic is the same for our strategy trip. Equipping a company with the right execution tools is like buying backpacks for a family. You don't want to overload the smaller units with too much weight. To succeed, they all need a backpack they can carry. *'One size fits all' doesn't work well on the execution road.* If we want to equip our travelers with better execution tools, we should make sure they fit. For example, a small unit of 200 people doesn't need the same BSC approach as one of 2,000. Sometimes, after a period of strong growth, the execution process might feel like a backpack that's too small. It might feel like the old execution process outgrew the company, like a kid who becomes a teenager and needs (wants) a real, grown-up backpack. But most of the time, it goes wrong because *we hand out execution backpacks that are way too big.* The message here isn't to offer made-to-measure backpacks. Strategists aren't into haut couture. Standardization is crucial. But we do want to offer our solution in a few different sizes. We want to offer a single brand Balanced Scorecard approach in 3 sizes: a light version for the small units, medium for the average-sized, and a full-blown one for the big units. Successful strategists design a standard, easy-to-use strategy execution process with matching tools and offer it in small, medium, and large.

4.
Tata's Dream

At Tata's research center in Mumbai, India, there were two cars on display. One was a complete prototype of the Nano—the $2,500 compact car they were working on. The other was a neat bi-section with the car's guts clearly visible.

Every day, people were invited to examine the car on display in the hope they would propose simplifications. It all started in 2003 with Ratan Tata's dream. He wanted to build the cheapest car in the world. He gave his engineering team, led by 32-year-old star engineer Girish Wagh, 3 requirements. The car should be dirt cheap, respect the regulatory safety requirements, and drive like a real car.

Their initial prototype didn't even come close. To keep costs down, the engineers had come up with a vehicle which had bars instead of doors, and plastic flaps to keep out the monsoon rains. It was closer to a quad cycle than a car and lacked punch. Even a bigger engine, which boosted the power by nearly 20 percent, was still dismal. "It was an embarrassment," Wagh admitted afterwards.

But, in hindsight, the first failure also proved to be very helpful. If they were to succeed in building a 'proper' car and not an upgraded four-wheel scooter or a cheap-looking alternative nobody would be interested in, they had to rethink every aspect of the car. They had to take each component—from the windshield wipers to the radio—and figure out what to leave and what to throw out. And for each component they decided to keep, they had to design it as simply as possible to keep the production costs under control. *The whole process was a balancing act.* Cutting too much or being too simplistic meant compromising on safety, performance, and design. Cutting too little meant a car that was too expensive.

To succeed in their tightrope act, they quickly understood they needed help. Ratan Tata called a meeting of his top parts suppliers and, after showing them the first flawed prototypes, asked them for support. At first, they were skeptical. But Tata persisted and, after some debate, most of Tata's regular suppliers joined the project. Rane Group, for example, focused on reducing the weight of the steering system materials used, replacing the steel rod of the steering with a steel tube—a major cost-reducer. Typically, the product is made of two pieces, but it was redesigned as one to save on machining and assembling costs. Another supplier, GKN Driveline's team, spent a year developing 32 experimental variants to create the perfect driveshaft—the component that transfers power from the engine to the wheel. With the help of their French and Italian designers, they changed the design to make it lighter and easier to manufacture.

Over time, Wagh's team grew to 500 engineers. A core team of 5 gathered every day at 3pm to discuss the latest developments. Each member represented a different part of the car—engine and transmission, body, vehicle integration, safety and regulation, and industrial design.

Fitting all the redesigned parts together was another challenge. The engine, for instance, had to be redesigned 3 times. Initially, Wagh thought they'd buy an off-the-shelf engine. The team evaluated all the small-capacity engines available, but found nothing suitable. So, in early 2005, they decided to build their own. The first was a 540cc engine that, when fitted on the prototype, lacked the necessary power. So its capacity was increased by 9 percent. But it still didn't deliver enough power. So they added another 9 percent before Wagh finally settled on a 623cc engine. This, however, required re-aligning the foot pedal to have sufficient legroom. And so on. In the end, the tightrope act paid off. When Ratan Tata stepped out of the driver's seat from the first Tata Nano, it made a lasting impression. What shook the automobile world most was the fact that the designers seemed to have done the impossible. The car was dirt cheap, but didn't look like it. *It didn't look like an upgraded 4-wheel scooter.* Instead, it was a nice-looking, real car... but with the price tag of a scooter.

5.
The Simplicity Tightrope

The challenges these engineers faced are comparable with those we face when we decide to combat CO$_2$mplexity. As with the Nano, we have to ask ourselves which process components we need and which can be left out. We should ask questions like, "Do we really need Balanced Scorecard software?" and "Do we really need to keep tracking those KPI's?" Or "Do we really need to include the corporate values as evaluation criteria in our individual objective-setting process?"

Our next challenge is to simplify, as far as possible, those components that we decide to keep. Einstein understood this challenge perfectly. He said, "We need to make things simple, but not too simple." To combat the CO$_2$mplexity villain, we need s*mart simplicity*. To combat CO$_2$mplexity, we have to make things simple. We have to ask ourselves questions like, "We have to manage projects, but do we need all the bells and whistles from the 100-page manual for every project?" and "We have a KPI dashboard, but do we need all those KPI's?" But we can't make things too simple. They still need to serve their purpose, like the size of the engine to keep speed and real doors for safety and comfort. We can probably simplify our budget process, but we do need its core. We can probably get rid of some of the complexity of our project management process, but we do need to manage our projects in a professional way. I'm sure you get the picture. Successful strategists walk *The Simplicity Tightrope*, carefully balancing the overly simple and the overly complex. Tip over to the complex side and you'll fall in the complexity swamp. Tip over to the simple side and the value is lost.

■ ■ ■

The ambitions that strategists lay out for an organization almost always demand business growth. Few strategy documents carry the message "Let's become smaller." But business growth doesn't come cheap. Growth charges a complexity tax. More tools, more templates, new matrix structures, extra communication channels, heavier budget procedures, and risk management controls are all put in place to make up for the social glue that is lost when groups become bigger.

CO_2mplexity is a sneaky villain, a real Ninja. He approaches in total silence and attacks from the shadows. Often, we don't even see him coming before it's too late. One more document here, a few more KPI's there, an extra steering committee to track new projects, an added resource to monitor risk. But all these components pile up and create a static, unhealthy environment. A place where decision-making demands too much energy and people get side-tracked from the execution shortcut, forgetting all about the real purpose of the journey. The result? The finish line becomes a distant dream. The big idea that once inspired a whole team fades away, like the crumpled paper above Raju's bed, the monk who wanted to become a Zen master but got sidetracked on his journey.

To combat CO$_2$mplexity, we should follow Babauta's example and strive to become a 100 Things Company, cutting away all process steps, procedures, and tools we collected over the years, but don't really need. To combat CO$_2$mplexity, we should equip our units with an execution backpack they can carry. We have 3 sizes on sale—small, medium, and large. To combat CO$_2$mplexity, we should strive for smart simplicity, making things simple, but not too simple. We should walk the Simplicity Tightrope, like a bunch of brilliant engineers did, creating a $2,500 car that still looks, feels, and drives like a real car.

CHAPTER 10

Experience the Power of Habits

What was the first thing you did when you got out of bed this morning? Check your emails, take a shower or have some breakfast? Did you brush your teeth before or after eating? Tie your left or right shoe first? Which route did you take to work? Did you hold the steering wheel with your left, right or both hands? When you got to the office, did you grab a coffee or turn your computer on first? *New York Times'* journalist Charles Duhigg wanted to understand how habits work. He interviewed more than 300 experts and digested an incredible amount of academic studies. One of Duhigg's findings is quite surprising—most of the choices we make each day may feel like the product of well-considered decision-making. But they're not. They're habits. *And they justify 40 percent (!) of what we do.*

Remember the cookies and radish experiment? The 67 participants that were teased with freshly baked chocolate cookies? Half of the group was allowed to dig in and eat the cookies. The second group was asked to eat radishes instead. When they had to trace a geometrical figure, the cookie contestants kept going for 18 minutes, making 34 attempts to solve the puzzle. The radish group gave up after 8 minutes and 19 attempts. Their willpower dwindled. They gave in. Willpower Depletion also explains why 88 percent of people don't achieve their New Year's resolutions, why shopping is so tiring, and why most dieters succumb to temptation in the evening.

Habits are nature's way of combating Willpower Depletion. Habits help us to protect one of our body's limited resources—rational decision-making. Each decision we take demands mental strength and when there are too many decisions to take, our reserves run out. *We become tired.* By automating small, repetitive decisions—such as what we do first in the morning, how we drive to work or tie our shoe laces—we safeguard our mental energy. Here's how it works. At one point, faced with a new situation, we take the time to rationally evaluate the options and make a deliberate decision. Then, after several repetitions, the choice becomes natural, the decision is automated, a habit is created. Let's take an example. Imagine starting a new job. On your first day, you have to decide how to get there, when to leave your house to be on time, where to park, how to greet your new colleagues, where to take lunch, and when to leave the office. The result? You get home drained. But, after a while, routine kicks in. You've figured out what time to get up, you've tried and tested a few different routes, and you've figured out how to behave to fit in. Those small choices that your brain found challenging on day one don't require brain power anymore. They're automated.

1.
Group Habits, aka Culture

Ask 100 CEO's, "Is having the right company culture crucial to succeed in business?" and most will answer 'yes'. But putting the right culture in place is a major challenge. "Culture eats strategy for breakfast every day," management guru Peter Drucker said. To successfully complete our strategy journey, we have to tackle the culture change challenge. Let's start by finding out why strategy ends up on the breakfast menu so often.

We saw in Chapter 2 that the collection of small choices travelers take on the execution road has to be in line with the big choice *(the Mintzberg Pattern). A new big choice demands a new set of small choices.* For example, when Jef Schrauwen decided to reposition his company to focus exclusively on front doors, he needed to completely rethink how to design, produce, and sell products. The new strategy triggered a whole new set of small choices that had to be put in place to create a decision pattern.

To connect culture with strategy, let's use the same denominator—decisions. In doing so, we can define culture as *the existing set of small choices.* When someone says, "We need to change our culture to make our strategy a success", using our definition it becomes, "We need to change the 'old' decision set with a 'new' decision set in line with the new big choice." At Alcoa, for example, O'Neill's new idea required everyone to abandon old behavior. To present an accident prevention plan within 24 hours of an incident occurring, business unit presidents had to hear from their vice presidents as soon as it happened. To make that happen, VP's had to be in constant communication with their first line managers. And they, in turn, had to have a process in place to get the right people around the table, analyse the accident, and come up with a list of sensible improvement suggestions. Almost everything they were used to about communicating across the hierarchy had to be abandoned and replaced.

When strategy meets culture on the battlefield, strategy arrives with a clear disadvantage. And that's because new decisions demand willpower—a scarce resource—and existing ones don't. It's the same handicap we've seen when our New Year's resolutions encounter daily life. If we want to avoid the same failure rate, if we want to avoid our strategy becoming a nice breakfast, we need to automate the crucial decisions that support our strategy as quickly as possible. That way, travelers don't tap into their willpower when they execute the new strategy. Only then can new choices replace old ones that don't fit the Mintzberg Pattern. Only then can our new strategy have the old culture for breakfast.

2.
How to Pick the Right Habits?

So what's the secret? How do we create new habits? And how do we make obsolete habits disappear? We learned in Chapter 5 that signposts tell us if we're on the right execution track or not (remember the Yasso 800?). *For each of these lead indicators, we should define a set of routines that shift them in the right direction.* If you're a marathon runner, you could include a weekly 800-meter training session in your program, add an extra weight-training session to strengthen specific muscle groups or tweak your diet for training days. Installing these routines will help you run a faster 800 meters (and ultimately help you reach the finish line of your next marathon faster).

Some routines have a spillover effect. Research shows, for example, that building the 'exercise' habit triggers all sorts of other positive routines. When people start to exercise, even only once a week, they start eating better, become more productive, smoke less, are more patient with colleagues and family, and use their credit cards less frequently. *The exercise habit has clear, positive spillover effects.* In his book, Charles Duhigg gives more examples:

> Studies have documented that families who habitually eat dinner together seem to raise children with better homework skills, higher grades, greater emotional control, and more confidence. Making your bed every morning is correlated with better productivity, a greater sense of well-being, and stronger skills at sticking with a budget. It's not that the family meal or a tidy bed *causes* better grades or less frivolous spending. But somehow those initial shifts start chain reactions that help other good habits take hold.

It's also good to know that we have many more existing routines than we think. Take eating, for example. Every day, we make all sorts of decisions about eating. We decide when to eat, what to eat, how much to eat. At work, we might decide to skip lunch. In the evening, we choose between eating out, ordering in, using the microwave or cooking from scratch. But because many of our habits are unconscious, *we're unaware of how many decisions we actually make.* Just try this little test. How many food-related decisions did you make in the last 24 hours?

Two professors from Cornell University, Brian Wansink and Jeffery Sobal, wanted to find the answer. They asked 154 students the same question. The answer? On average, the students indicated they made 14.4 daily food-related decisions. This sounds like a reasonable number right? But then both researchers pushed the students to think a bit harder. They were asked to analyze their eating pattern in the same way a good journalist approaches an article using questions related to the who, what, where, when, and how. For example, when do you start and stop eating? Who's with you? Where do you eat? How much do you eat? Some students were also given a clicker that they had to push every time they made a food-related decision.

Now, the students were able to guess far more accurately. And the results were mind-blowing. Using the more thorough approach, they counted 226.7 (!) daily food-related decisions—*15 times more than their initial guess.* This study is a good illustration of how most of our habits fly under the radar. *If we want to change the culture in our organization, we first have to find the habits that define our culture.*

3.
The Nun and the CEO

During an Alcoa shareholder meeting in Pittsburg, a Benedictine nun called Sister Mary Margaret, stood up and accused Paul O'Neill of lying. She said that while they were bragging about their safety measures, workers at the Alcoa plant in Mexico were becoming sick because of dangerous fumes.

O'Neill firmly disagreed. He promptly pulled up a graph on his laptop to illustrate the excellent safety records from the Mexico plant. On top of that, Robert Barton, the executive in charge of the facility, was a highly respected leader at Alcoa. He had been with the company for decades and was responsible for some of their largest partnerships.

But despite all the evidence, the nun told the audience they shouldn't trust the CEO before she sat down.

To be safe, O'Neill asked the HR director to fly to Mexico to find out what was going on. On site in Mexico, they went through the plant's records and found proof of an accident. A few months before, there had been a build-up of fumes inside the building. *But Barton never reported the incident.*

Once back in Pittsburg, during the briefing, O'Neill asked, "Did Barton know that people got sick?" "We didn't meet with him," was the answer. "But yeah, it's pretty clear he knew."

Two days later, Barton was fired.

Wasn't this punishment over the top, as many outsiders thought? Why fire one of your best people for a rather minor safety incident? But, at Alcoa, firing Barton was the logical consequence of their choice to become a zero accident company. "Barton fired himself," said one of his colleagues, "there wasn't even a choice."

To succeed, Alcoa needed new routines. And one of the most important habits needing adoption was a fast loop to learn from their mistakes. Therefore, everyone was required to report incidents with a matching improvement plan within 24 hours. Without this, they would never become the safe company they wanted to be. The way Barton was treated was a logical consequence of that choice. "It might have been hard at another company to fire someone who had been there so long. It wasn't hard for me," O'Neill explained afterwards. "Barton got fired because he didn't report the incident and so no one else had the opportunity to learn from it. Not sharing an opportunity to learn is a cardinal sin." In other words, Barton wasn't fired because of the accident. He was fired because of his behavior *afterwards*. His choice not to report the incident didn't fit the overall decision pattern. In fact, it went completely against it, preventing crucial habits from forming. *(If a top executive doesn't have to report an incident, then why would I?)*

In order to develop new habits like O'Neill's 'report within 24 hours', it's crucial to act strongly against behavior that disrupts the pattern. Successful strategists identify and fight against decision pattern disruption. They act against unacceptable small choices because they know that wrong behavior prevents cultivating the right habits. If we all agree to drive on the right side of the road, we have to take action against people who choose to drive on the left. Because once a few people start doing the wrong thing, others start copying it. Not necessarily because they want to be disruptive, but because it's often the easy thing to do—or worse because they think it's the right thing to do. And before long, there's chaos. Successful strategists ask, "What are unacceptable small choices on the execution road?" and take strong action when they occur, even if this seems illogical to the outside world.

■ ■ ■

So far, we've learned that our strategy journey becomes easier when we automate repetitive, small decisions. Habits keep our willpower reserve maxed out, making sure our strategy doesn't end up as a nice breakfast snack. We've also learned which decisions we should automate, those choices that positively impact our lead indicators—our finish line signposts. And we've learned that it's important to act resolutely against people who take deliberate decisions that go against building the right habits. Like O'Neill did. The CEO fired one of his best executives because he chose not to report a safety issue, a deadly sin at Alcoa.

But there's one question that remains unanswered. *How do we develop execution habits?* How do we transform small, repetitive decisions into routines? In our search for the answer, we'll travel to the South Pole—a destination where one wrong decision, even a small one, can make the difference between life and death.

CHAPTER 11

Find Your 7-day Rhythm

T he South Pole is one of Earth's final frontiers. A barren environment covered in 5 million square miles of ice. A destination that inspires adventurers to embark on epic journeys that challenge the boundaries of human endurance and strength. Dixie Dansercoer is such an adventurer. He made his first trip to Greenland when he was 31. Since then, the ice has kept calling and Dansercoer has launched himself into various polar adventures. He made the first crossing of the Arctic Ocean over the North Pole to Greenland, sailed in the footsteps of Adrien de Gerlache exactly 100 years after his famous expedition, and made an aborted crossing of the Bearing Strait due to ice breakup and dangerous weather conditions.

In 2008, Dansercoer dreamed of a new polar expedition—a challenge more demanding than anything he'd ever done before. *He wanted to complete the longest unsupported Antarctica journey.* To succeed, he would have to pull a 440lb sled with enough supplies for 3,738 miles, face an average daily temperature of -29°F (-34°C), sleep in a tent only a few degrees warmer, and kite ski for 10 to 12 hours a day—a feat that would require effort equal to an Ironman triathlon on a daily basis.

When it comes to such an extreme challenge, split-second decision-making is crucial. On a previous expedition, Dixie fell through the ice. With the water at just 28.7°F (-1.8°C), he would die from hypothermia in minutes. But thanks to preparation for such as incident and the quick thinking of his traveling companion Alain Hubert, he got out and survived. Another time, a noise woke him up in the thick of night. It took just a few seconds to realize they were in immediate danger. A hungry polar bear with cubs stood menacingly at the front of their tent. Instinctively, they grabbed the gun from the right pocket of the tent and, with a grazing shot, scared them away. Because of the unique decisions that such conditions demand, polar adventurers make sure they don't have to worry about small, repetitive decisions. Instead, they develop their own particular routines. "You have to program yourself as a robot," Dixie said to me. "It's the only way to survive in these extreme conditions."

■ ■ ■

On November 4 2011 after a 6.5-hour flight from Cape Town, Dansercoer and his fellow traveler Sam Deltour set foot on the ice in Antarctica. They took along 100 daily food rations, 6.9 gallons of fuel, one tent, 6 kites each, a sleeping bag, a repair kit, a first aid kit, their daily journal, a motivational book, a satellite phone, scientific research tools, some spare clothes, and one immense map of Antarctica.

From Day one, Dansercoer and Deltour followed a strict daily rhythm. "Once on the ice, it's crucial to get your routines up and running as fast as possible," Dansercoer explained. "And I've learned that it works best when you stick to a strict, predefined schedule." Due to the contrast between the outside temperature and the body's sleep state, it's most critical to quickly establish a morning ritual (to avoid freezing to death while your body is heating up to face the cold). Dansercoer's day starts at 6.30am. He gets dressed quickly in his pre-laid out clothes, empties the pee bottle, brushes ice crystals off the tent, starts the small cooking stove, collects snows for melting, wakes up Sam, sticks his nose outside the tent to gauge weather conditions, chooses his outer clothing for the day, fills a thermos, drinks tea, takes a toilet break, eats breakfast, jokes with Sam, cleans up, analyzes the weather conditions, and decides on the best plan for the day. Together, they throw their bags out, load the sleds, take down the tent, and prepare the kites. On a very cold morning, this routine includes a jog to get the blood pumping.

Dansercoer knows all about the power of habits. It saves time, frees up brain power, and facilitates teamwork. And he knows how to put them in place according to a predefined structure—a rhythm. At the start of the expedition, it took them 3 hours to complete their morning ritual. Every decision was a conscious one that needed willpower. But after a while, routine kicked in and they did it in 90 minutes—a 50 percent time gain.

Dansercoer isn't the only polar adventurer to stick to a rhythm. In 1911, 2 expedition teams were on a quest to be the first people in modern history to reach the South Pole. One group was led by Norwegian Roald Amundsen and the other by Robert Falcon Scott. After weeks of hardship, challenges, and acute dangers, Amundsen's team arrived first. More than a month later, Scott's team also made it. But because of logistical mistakes, exhaustion, bad weather, and a shortage of supplies, they never made it back. Author Roland Huntford studied every detail of both men and their journeys to the South Pole. He found that the daily rhythm was one of the key reasons why Amundsen made it...

and Scott didn't.

1.
Implementation Intentions

A few days before the Christmas vacation, Professor Peter Gollwitzer asked his students for help. He told them he was studying how people spent their holidays. And to get the necessary information, he asked them to write a report on how they spent Christmas Eve. To receive credits, it had to be written and emailed to the researchers no later than 48 hours afterwards.

In reality, Gollwitzer wasn't interested in their holiday activities. He wanted to find out how people deal with goals when there are lots of distractions. And what better way than to give a group of students an assignment with a tight deadline during their vacation?

One group of students didn't get any more instructions and went off to celebrate their holiday. The second group got an extra question-naire on which they had to fill in exactly when and where they were going to write the report in those critical 48 hours.

Now, just imagine you're one of those students. You arrive home after a tough semester. It's Christmas. You have time to catch up with family and friends. The fire's lit, presents are under the tree, and there are home-cooked meals, a few drinks, and siblings to challenge you at a PlayStation game. Would you put these to one side to write your report?

The answer? If you wrote down a specific time and place to com-plete the paper, you probably would. Gollwitzer and his research team found that specific cues—what he calls '*implementation intentions*'—help individuals take action. In the experiment, the students from the second group had to write down the specific time and place they would write the report. For example, "I'm going to write my report before breakfast on December 26 in my old bedroom." Of the first group, only 33 percent managed to complete the assignment on time. But of the individuals from the group that used implementation intentions—those that wrote down a specific time and place—75 percent wrote the report.

Hundreds of subsequent studies have since confirmed Gollwitzer's findings. Specific cues to when and where you are going to take action have a positive effect on actually getting things done. *Implementation intentions work.* And they work particularly well when we face a difficult challenge, as a group of 68-year-old patients discovered while recovering from hip surgery.

Two researchers wanted to test the strength of implementation intentions in difficult situations. To do so, they walked into a hospital and recruited a group of patients that were undergoing hip surgery. What you have to know is that the recovery process of such a medical procedure is quite challenging. The pain will get worse before it gets better. So, it's not hard to understand that patients don't like to do what the doctor ordered because of the pain they inflict on themselves. Even if they knew the pain will help them to recover faster and avoid developing life-threatening blood clots.

After their surgery, one group of patients received a booklet that explained the 3-month recovery process in detail. It also contained a section where they could write down exactly what they were going to do. For instance, "If you are going to go for a walk this week, please write down when and where you plan to walk." *These patients were asked to set implementation intentions for the actions they wanted to take to recover.* The results were quite dramatic. On average, those patients that worked with the booklet were bathing themselves 4 weeks faster, getting out of bed 6 weeks earlier, and standing up after 3.5 weeks instead of 7.7.

In general, scientific research proves that when we face an easy task, defining when and where we are going to do it increases its success rate by around 10 percent. But when we face a difficult challenge, using implementation intentions will increase our success rate by a whopping 300 percent. *Implementation intentions triple our mileage on the execution road.*

According to Gollwitzer, implementation intentions have such a positive impact because they help us *pre-load difficult decisions.* "By forming implementation intentions, people strategically switch from conscious effortful control of their goal-directed behavior to being automatically controlled by situational cues," he points out. In other words, we take the rational decision upfront, when we put the when and where in our agenda. And when time comes to take action, our agenda protects us from backing out.

Have you noticed the important difference between an implementation intention and an action? An action identifies *what* you need to do to reach the finish line. An implementation intention is a specific commitment to *when and where* you're taking action. In short, *an implementation intention is an action cue.* And as we learned from Gollwitzer, adding an action cue to an action makes all the difference—especially when we know we have to take action but find it hard to do so, like a colleague student who wants to earn extra credits with a report she has to write during her holiday, a 68-year-old patient who wants to recover but fears the pain or an adventurer who wants to cross Antarctica but faces incredible hardships.

2.
Strategy Anchors

So far, in our search to understand how to develop habits on our strategy journey, we've learned that implementation intentions are crucial to getting difficult things done. These 'when and where' cues help get things done by pre-loading tough execution decisions.

We've also learned that habits are born of repetition. If we want to automate the small decisions that move our lead indicators, we also need to repeat the cue over and over again. Once the actions to move lead indicators are identified, travelers have to specify *when and where they're going to take action on a repetitive basis*. They need to install an execution rhythm, like Dixie Dansercoer. In *Making Habits, Breaking Habits*, Jeremy Dean tells the following story:

> A young comedian asked Jerry Seinfeld, the famous comedian, for advice on how to improve. Seinfeld replied that the key to being a better comedian was to write better jokes, and the way to write better jokes was to practice. But it wasn't just about practicing in general, Seinfeld explained. It was about building up a habit—the writing habit. Seinfeld advised using a simple trick to get the habit going. You buy a big wall calendar with a box for every day of the year. Then, each day that you complete your writing task, you put a big cross on the calendar. As the weeks pass, the chain of crosses on the calendar grows longer and longer. Your only job, advised Seinfeld, was not to break the chain. *He urged the young comedian to develop a rhythm.*

Repetitive weekly cues that help automate execution decisions are called *Strategy Anchors*. They help us take on the villain Willpower Depletion during the time that habits remain unformed or fragile. These anchors ensure that our good intentions on the road to success aren't blown away by day-to-day distractions, competing destinations or existing bad habits. You might have spotted that I suggest a weekly rhythm, while Dansercoer and Seinfeld favor a daily one. It's true that a daily rhythm creates habits faster—but in my experience, a daily schedule is unrealistic in most business environments. A 7-day rhythm however gives you the benefit of regular repetitions, while following a more natural business flow. As the authors of the *The 4 Disciplines of Execution* nicely point out, "In many operating environments, weeks represent a natural rhythm or organizational life. We think in weeks. We talk in weeks. They have beginnings and ends. They are the staple of human condition and make for a perfect cadence of accountability."

The Strategy Anchors don't have to dominate the agenda. But they have to be there, week after week, month after month. There will be times when travelers face tempting distractions, like those students during their Christmas vacations. There will be times, especially at the start, when they wonder if it's all worth it. There will be times when travelers are swamped with work and don't really have the time. *But the user manual for strategy anchors is very simple.* If someone, for whatever reason, removes an anchor from their agenda, they need to re-attach it in that same week. Many a Sunday, I've ended up catching up on the 90-minute writing blocks that I'd skipped during the other 6 days of the week. But I never broke the 7-day rhythm, as I knew that it would be the end of my writing journey. Remove the anchor and the ship is lost. Strategy becomes like a shipwreck bobbing on the waves, destined to end up far from the finish line.

Luckily, after some time, the power of a habit kicks in and the Strategy Anchors grow stronger. And if you keep going, they're so engrained that you respond automatically to the cue, as Alcoa executives experienced. One related a story of him watching some guys from his office window working on a bridge without using the proper safety procedures. He went down 5 flights of stairs and went and told these guys they were risking their lives. When he was told their supervisor hadn't brought the equipment, he called the local Occupational Safety and Health Administration office and turned the supervisor in. Another executive told a story about him stopping at a street excavation near his house and lecturing the workers for not having a trench box. Deciding to stop to address a bunch of workers on the weekend with his kids in the car isn't normal behavior. *We wouldn't naturally decide to do it.* But that's the point. The Alcoa safety habit took over. Habits are a force of nature. And we too can take advantage of their power on our strategy journey. We just have to follow nature's logic to create a habit. And the logic is this: Strategy Anchors force repetition. Repetition creates routines. Routines beat Willpower Depletion. Hands take over from the head. And the activity, once experienced as extremely difficult, becomes second nature. A habit is born.

■ ■ ■

The first 10 days of the expedition, Dansercoer and Deltour didn't progress quite as planned. A mega storm created abnormally high sastrugi (sharp, irregular ridges formed by wind erosion) in the area where they started their journey. Progress against a stormy headwind was so painstakingly slow that there had to be two to pull one sled, going back and fore between sleds. After a week, they should've covered 260 miles. They only did 16. Would this be the end of their journey? Their headquarters got in touch with Irina Gorodetskaya, a scientist specializing in meteorological conditions in Antarctica. The only option, she said, was to restart from an area where the storm wasn't impacting the terrain so much. After careful deliberation, taking a risk with the financial implications, Dansercoer and Deltour decided to go for it. They knew they wouldn't be able to complete the loop with their remaining food stocks. But if they could stick to their initially planned daily effort, they might still be able to break the record.

Their decision paid off. And although the terrain was still quite rough, it was less hostile than before. They were able to use their kites and made good progress. On Day 30, they reached their first milestone, the South Pole. "A small victory," Dixie wrote in his journal, "even if we still have a very long road ahead of us. But those are worries for later. Now, it's time to celebrate."

3.
From Strategy to...

The findings presented in the last 2 chapters have 3 important consequences for the way we look at successful strategy journeys. First of all, the phrase *'from strategy to action'*—often used to describe good strategy execution—is a dangerous execution mantra. It leads us to think that actions are the end station, the last step in the strategy cascade. But they're not. Research shows us that even if we pick the right actions, there's a big chance nothing will happen due to Willpower Depletion. And that's especially true when getting things done is considered difficult. If we want to maximize our chance to reach the finish line, Strategy Anchors are a crucial complement to actions. We make our strategy journey a lot easier by anchoring small decisions into travelers' weekly schedules, setting up a rhythm that creates habits. Therefore, a better execution mantra should be *'from strategy to Strategy Anchors.'* Only when strategy finds itself into everyone's agenda and gets anchored will travelers beat the willpower villain and create new habits. Only when that happens can the obsolete culture be replaced by a collection of new habits that support the Mintzberg Pattern. Only when strategists introduce Strategy Anchors will travelers be able to follow the execution path all the way to the end.

Secondly, these findings challenge us to take a different look at the traditional time horizons that strategists use. When we contemplate the future, we often divide the future into 3 timeframes. Our first time horizon is situated at 5-to-15 years, looking at the long-term industry and consumer trends. The second outlook is 3-to-5 years, chasing after a unique industry position. The third is a yearly cycle, translating our ambition into operational targets. But if we follow the logic science presents us, we should add a fourth timeframe, one that feels quite counter-intuitive for a strategist. *We need to think in weeks.* Let's be absolutely clear. Thinking about a 7-day timeframe isn't the same as short-term thinking. The latter is focused on chronological time—tomorrow, next week or next month. The 7-day rhythm requires us to break down our strategy journey into a 7-day rhythm, as Dansercoer broke down his adventure into a daily rhythm. Successful strategists think about a 7-day rhythm for the different groups on the execution road. *And they do it long before the strategy journey starts.*

Finally, we should embrace the power of habits, tapping into this well of human strength. Over the course of this book, we have met quite a few villains such as Decision Paralysis, the Curse of Knowledge and Golem, who make progress on the execution road hard work. All of these human peculiarities make executing strategy an uphill journey, one that feels like pushing a big snowball up a steep hill. And with every step we take, the execution challenge gets bigger and bigger, more difficult to push to the top. But when we make the third connection, when we connect our strategy with the Hands, this time, human nature works in our favor. It's a fact of life that our rational decision power—our head—can't outrun the Willpower Depletion villain. But habits can. Habits are our trump card, our ace that beats all the others in the execution game. "Habits draw us irresistibly towards our destiny" said William James, the famous psychologist. Once travelers have the winning deck in their hands, we've reached the top of the hill. Once our strategy finds its way into travelers' hands, once small decisions become habits, the snowball can follow a downhill course to the finish line. Execution progress becomes automatic, human behavior takes over, and travelers are irresistibly drawn towards the finish line.

...

Back to the ice. On Day 32, the adventurers moved into uncharted territory. They still had 1,800 miles ahead of them. Over the next 30 days, they made excellent progress. But then fate struck again. The temperature dropped to dangerous levels. "Temperatures between -20 and -30 degrees are what you expect," Dixie said. "You have to be vigilant, but there's no immediate risk. But when the temperature drops below -30 degrees and the wind is blowing fiercely, you play Russian Roulette. One wrong decision will hit you hard." *And it did.*

It was -41°C on Day 64. But the wind was good so they decided to go for it. During a short break, Dixie told Sam his cheek felt strange. For Sam, this was a clear warning sign as his travel companion never complained. And it turned out his fears were founded. Dansercoer's cheek had between second to third-degree frostbite. It had never happened before. At the same time, Sam had his own problems. The constant ski kiting was taking its toll. His ankle was infected and he could barely walk. Should they abort the mission? They decided to treat their wounds and give it one final try. In the meantime, they would prepare for evacuation in case it didn't work. Deltour's medical training proved very useful. He injected above and below his ankle a shot of cortisone he had brought for emergencies and treated Dansercoer's frostbite with aloe vera. Their tenacity paid off. They kept going, slowly, but surely. And on a stormy February day, Dixie Dansercoer and Sam Deltour reached 69° 33' 24 S / 93° 36' 20 E. After a grueling 74-day journey, both Antarctic travelers crossed their finish line. They became the first humans to travel 3,114 miles across the South Pole, opening up a new route in East Antarctica.

CHAPTER 12

The H³-connector

Over the course of *The Execution Shortcut*, we've looked at several successful idea journeys. Think about Paul O'Neill's crazy idea that transformed a sluggish aluminum company into a top performer. Think about Donald Berwick's bold idea that motivated doctors and nurses all over the world to save 100,000+ lives. Or think about Stephen Denning's impossible idea that converted the World Bank into a global knowledge management player. All of these journeys have one thing in common. Only when people started to care about the idea did something start to happen. This is the first lesson of the Execution Shortcut. It's the Heart Connection that kick-starts travelers. *It's the emotional bond with an idea that motivates people to contribute, not the brilliance of the idea itself.* This comes as a surprise. Most of us go for a Head approach to convince others of our great idea. We look for best practices, compile a few well-selected graphs, list all the benefits, and arrange our findings in a smart PowerPoint presentation. We think, "Once they understand our idea, they will help us." But when there's a lot of uncertainty, people are reluctant to change. They don't want to move. To overcome this inertia and kick-start travelers, strategists should aim for the heart first.

There are several tactics to conquer hearts. First, we can uncover a great story and wrap it around our big idea, just like Stephen Denning did. He picked up the Zambia story during a casual discussion in the canteen and wrapped it around his idea. His Zambia story shifted the executives' mindset on knowledge management from a rational "Do I agree or not with the idea?" to an emotional "Why don't we do this?" Remember Bob Ocwieja too. He spotted Jared's story—the obese college student who started eating fast food to lose weight. It proved to be an excellent wrapper around the idea, 'You can eat healthily at Subway.'

We can also tweak the environment to boost micro-commitment. Think about Peter's story. We shouldn't settle for small commitments on big things, but go after big commitments on small things. We should offer Big Yeses only and challenge others to do the same. We can help others climb the Micro-commitment Ladder by making 'no' an acceptable alternative for the fake yeses. Just think about the amazing success stories in cockpits and emergency rooms. Travelers, just like nurses and co-pilots, can effectively challenge decisions. They just have to learn how.

And we can boost belief. We've seen that it's possible to make runners run faster, soldiers to fight better, and natives to beat immigrants. Surprisingly, the key to success is belief. Roger Bannister ran the race of the century because he believed he could. Sixteen runners ran the race of their lives because they started to believe. A bunch of soldiers outperformed others only because their instructor believed they could. Success is a self-fulfilling prophecy. When we believe, our minds and bodies gather resources to dig deeper, recover faster, and keep going longer. When others believe in us, the dynamic is rein-forced. Think about the Israeli soldiers. Their instructors' beliefs made them better soldiers. Like the native workers in the factory, they had the ability to succeed. They only needed someone who believed in them so they could believe in themselves.

But travelers can't complete the strategy journey on motivation alone. In order to make sound day-to-day decisions, they need to un-derstand your idea. If strategy is a decision pattern, strategy execution is enabling people to create a decision pattern. This notion requires a big shift in the way we think about execution. As a strategist looking at strategy execution, we should imagine a decision tree rather than an action plan. This is the second lesson of the Execution Shortcut. *Decision patterns are at the core of successful strategy journeys, not to-do lists.* To improve execution speed and accuracy, we should shift our energy from asking people to make action plans to helping them make better decisions.

The start of a strategy journey is marked by a big choice—a deci-sion about the 'who' and 'how'. The end is a finish line—a destination postcard capturing the core of the big choice and showing travelers in an inspiring way what strategy success looks like. In between the start and finish, day-to-day decisions play a key role. These SMALL choic-es need to be in line with the big choice in order to create a path, a Mintzberg Pattern. Successful strategists facilitate these small choices using 4 tactics. They provide a List of Noes to limit the options, just like we learned from Michael Porter. They provide a Decision Intent for the remaining options, just like Alexandre Behring's 5 simple rules that put a Brazilian railway company back on track. They keep the big choice free from Strategy Graffiti, just like brand managers who pro-tect their brand. And finally, they provide a set of finish line signposts to keep everyone on the right path—just like Billy Beane's sabermet-rics showed his team the road to success.

But even when travelers stick to the right path, their autonomous travel radius is limited. Even if they want to (they care) and they have the right decision information (they understand), then efforts will stop after a few weeks. Not because they don't want to, but because they ran out of gas. Their willpower is depleted. This is the third lesson of the Execution Shortcut. *The human ability to make rational decisions is limited.* This explains why 88 percent of all New Year's resolutions don't make it to February, why participants who get radishes instead of cookies give up 50 percent faster, and why great action plans end up collecting dust on a shelf.

Luckily, there are ways to increase travelers' autonomy on the execution road. Like Ratan Tata's 500 engineers, you can walk the Simplicity Tightrope, creating a working environment where CO_2mplexity doesn't slow down decisions. Like Dixie Dansercoer, you can take advantage of the power of habits to outwit Willpower Depletion. You just have to follow nature's logic. And the logic is this: Strategy Anchors force repetition. Repetition creates routines. Routines beat Willpower Depletion. Hands take over from the head. And the activity, once experienced as extremely difficult, becomes second nature. An execution habit is born.

IN THE END, STRATEGY SUCCESS largely depends on the strategist's ability to make successful H^3-connections. And while the need for this triple connection is obvious—so obvious most idea creators don't think twice about it—successful H^3-connections are much harder to make than most of us think. Not so much about *who* we are, but because of *how* we are programmed as human beings. When our idea—whether it's a corporate strategy, a business plan for a new product launch or a policy to improve the education system—comes into contact with million-year-old human dynamics, our idea is in trouble. If we want people to understand our idea, we have to overcome the Curse of Knowledge. If we want people to make the right choices, we have to combat the villain Decision Paralysis. If we want to keep the core of our idea visible, we have to fight Message Distortion. If we want others to challenge questionable decisions, we have to circumvent Mitigated Speech. If we want the whole team to perform at peak level, we should tackle Golem. If we want to speed up decisions, we should reduce CO_2mplexity. And if we want people to keep pushing our idea forward, we have to outwit Willpower Depletion. *These powerful human complexities make strategy journeys extremely challenging.* They also explain why most strategies take the long road to the finish line. Or worse, never make it at all.

But if there is difficulty on the execution road, there is a large measure of hope as well. Simply by wrapping a story around our big idea, adopting a crew concept, and boosting belief, we can motivate others. By providing prioritization support, a finish line and a few well-chosen signposts, we can improve decisiveness. By simplifying the working environment and cultivating the right execution habits, we can energize travelers. And that's great news. *It means we can influence the path our strategy takes.* It means we can greatly improve the odds of strategy success in our favor. In the end, traveling the Execution Shortcut means tapping into the hidden potential we all have as human beings. So why not tap into this well of human strength? Why not be a H[3]-connector? Connect your strategy with the Hearts, Heads, and Hands of your fellow travelers and uncover the hidden path to success.

SHORTCUT
RESOURCES

THE EXECUTION SHORTCUT

Why Some Strategies Take the Hidden Path to Success and Others Never Reach the Finish Line

This book has covered a lot of ground. Here are a few resources to help prompt your memory or start a discussion.

Twitter Summary

Most strategies get lost on the long road to success. Connect your strategy with Heads, Hearts & Hands to uncover *The Execution Shortcut*.

The Elevator Pitch

The strategy journey to success is long and dangerous. Most strategies lose between 40 and 60 percent of their financial potential along the execution highway. There is a path that will make the trip dramatically shorter. It exists in every organization, but mostly stays hidden. With the help of science, we'll uncover *The Execution Shortcut*. There are three prerequisites: (1) The Head connection—people need to be aware of your strategy; (2) The Heart connection—people need to care about your strategy; (3) The Hands connection—people need the energy to push your strategy forwards.

One-page Summary

On page 155, you'll find 25 key ideas summarized on a single page.

The Shortcut Map

On page 156, you'll find the book summarized in drawings. See if you can spot 25 key messages from the book. (You'll find some hints on page 158).

Bob the Strategy Tourist

Sometimes an image says more than a thousand words. On my blog—www.jeroen-de-flander.com—you can download a number of cartoons to use and share.

The Shortcut Discussion Guide

The days of authors getting the last word are over. That's your privilege. Now that you've finished this book, go out and laud it on your blog, on Twitter or your favorite social networking site. Or, if you really want to make the ideas from *The Execution Shortcut* come alive, talk them over with some colleagues, friends or at your book club. On my blog—www.jeroen-de-flander.com—you will find 20 questions to get the conversation going.

How to Take an Execution Shortcut

CENTRAL QUESTION	Why do some strategies take the hidden path to success and others never reach the finish line?
ANSWER	Human dynamics—the execution villains—are the reason why most strategies take the long route to the finish line. If we aspire to get a better return from our strategy, then we must learn how these human behaviors impact the idea journey and how to deal with them. In short, we need a H^3-connection.

HEAD — **PEOPLE NEED TO BE AWARE OF YOUR STRATEGY**

› *Facilitate SMALL choices.* Provide prioritization guidelines to align day-to-day choices with the big choice (Lisa's Dilemma, Michael Porter's No, Railway)

› *Keep the Big Choice Clearly Visible.* Keep the original big choice clearly visible (The Tripping Point, A Horse is Not a Zebra)

› *Draw a Finish Line.* Capture the core of your strategy and show everyone in an inspiring way what strategy success looks like (200 Doors, Man on the Moon)

› *Re-measure.* Provide a compact measurement set and remove useless signposts (Yasso 800, Billy Beane, Players Versus Coach)

HEART — **PEOPLE NEED TO CARE ABOUT YOUR STRATEGY**

› *Share Strategy Stories.* Add context and emotion to the strategy to make people feel the big choice (The Kidney Heist, The Zambia Story, Jared's Diet)

› *Climb the Micro-commitment Ladder.* Don't settle for small commitments on big things. Go after big commitments on small things (5 x Yes, Hospitals and Cockpits)

› *Go Beyond Self-interest.* Celebrate small victories on the road, making people believe in a big victory at the finish line (Bannister, Pygmalion and Golem)

HANDS — **PEOPLE NEED ENERGY TO DRIVE YOUR STRATEGY**

› *Tackle CO$_2$mplexity.* Embrace simplicity and create a productive working environment (The Last Zen Master, Tata's Dream, The Simplicity Tightrope)

› *Experience the Power of Habits.* Automate small decisions to save energy (Nun and CEO, Strategy Eats Culture)

› *Find Your 7-day Rhythm.* Connect decision horizons: find a spot for strategy in everyone's weekly agenda (South Pole Expedition, Hip Surgery, Strategy Anchors).

The Shortcut Map

From the book *The Execution Shortcut* by Jeroen De Flander.

Illustrator: Paul Verhoestraete

The Shortcut Map

Notes

2   **Paul O'Neill story.** See Charles Duhigg's (2012) excellent book, *The Power of Habit.*

3   **100,000 Lives Campaign.** I drew from several sources for Donald Berwick's story including Alice G. Gosfield and James L. Reinertsen, The 100,000 Lives Campaign: *Crystallizing Standards Of Care For Hospitals (Health Affairs).* Chip and Dan Heath, *Switch.* Hayagreeva Rao and Robert Sutton, "The Ergonomics of Innovation", *McKinsey Quarterly.* Website of the Institute for Healthcare Improvement, http://www.ihi.org/Pages/default.aspx.

3   **4,050 hospitals.** Eight states enrolled 100 percent of their hospitals in the Campaign and 18 states enrolled over 90 percent of their hospitals in the Campaign. More info on the IHI website, http://www.ihi.org.

7   **The Curse of Knowledge.** Colin Camerer, George Loewenstein

and Mark Weber (1989), "The Curse of Knowledge in Economic Settings: An Experimental Analysis", *Journal of Political Economy* 97: 1232–1254. Chip and Dan Heath, "The Curse of Knowledge", *Harvard Business Review.*

8   **The E Experiment.** See Adam Galinsky (2008), *The 'E' and 'Fan' Experiments*, CNBC.

9   **The Jam Experiment.** See Iyengar, S. (Columbia) and Lepper, M. (Stanford) (2000), "When choice is demotivating: Can one desire too much of a good thing?", *Journal of Personality and Social Psychology*, 79, 995-1006.

10 **The Cookies Experiment.** Roy F. Baumeister, Ellen Bratslavsky, Mark Muraven, and Dianne M. Tice, "Ego Depletion: Is the Self a Limited Resource?", *Journal of Personality and Social Psychology* (1998), Vol 74, No 5, 1252-1265.

12 *the performance factory* **research.** *The Strategy Execution Barometer – Expanded Edition* (2012).

CHAPTER 2

21 **Mintzberg's insights.** Henry Mintzberg (May 1978), "Patterns in Strategy Formulation", *Management Science*, Vol. 24, No 9, pp934-948.

21 **Basic strategy stuff.** A great book to get up to speed on strategy is *Understanding Michael Porter*, Joan Magretta (2012), Harvard Business Review Press.

22 **Britney Gallivan of Pomona.** You can read Gallivan's story on the Pomona Valley website, http://pomonahistorical.org/12times. htm. The challenge has also been addressed on the Math World website, http://mathworld.wolfram.com/Folding.html.

23 **Next Generation Strategy event.** This event took place on October 12 2010 in Cairo, Egypt. Roger Martin and Costas Markides spoke on the first day. Michael and I shared the stage on Day 2.

You can download my presentation from SlideShare http://www.slideshare.net/Jeroendeflander.

24 **Shared Value.** The central idea behind creating Shared Value is that the competitiveness of a company and the health of the communities around it are mutually dependent. In other words, it's possible to enhance the competitive position of a company while at the same time advancing the society in which it operates. For an interesting article, see *Harvard Business Review* (2011), "Creating Shared Value: Redefining Capitalism and the Role of the Corporation in Society" by Michael Porter and Mark R. Kremer. I believe Shared Value is an interesting way to look differently at Corporate Social Responsibility. In my previous book, I wrote about the three generations of CSR. The first CSR generation is made up of 'Donators.' They are good citizens who believe in the traditional trade-off between organizations and society, but want to give something back to society to compensate. The second CSR generation is made up of the 'Avoiders.' Their main objective is to reduce any negative impact of their own activities. Avoiders are aware that certain activities from their value chain have a negative impact on society and they try to reduce the negative impact. The third CSR generation are the 'Creators.' This group embraces the Shared Value concept and view sustainability as a positive sum game. They see Corporate Social Responsibility as an investment, not an expense. Want more info? You can download a presentation from SlideShare http://www.slideshare.net/Jeroendeflander.

24 **List of Noes (1).** Here are 2 questions to spark a List of Noes discussion: "Which customers in our industry do we make unhappy?" and "Where did we systematically deliver a clear 'no' last year?"

List of Noes (2). The most interesting noes are the old yeses—the products and services you have been offering so far, but you don't want to offer any more. Here's how Jef Schrauwen formulated one of his noes: "We'd been offering all kinds of carpenting products to all kinds of clients. Basically, we made what clients asked us to make. But now we sell front doors and say no to windows, shutters, and pool houses."

List of Noes (3). Strategists draw a realistic List of Noes. A company isn't always in a position to say 'no' from one day to the next. There will be future noes that are still needed today to keep the company up and running. In the short run, Jef knew his company couldn't make the switch to producing only front doors. Therefore, he added, "When our backlog drops below 12 weeks, we will offer other products to clients that order a front door." Unless a company sells its core activities to generate cash for developing the new business, it probably needs to manage the transition period by including *yeses in transition* on the List of Noes.

21 **Big choice.** A big choice is always relative to the rules of the industry and what others are doing. It's not set in stone. It's also good to know that the average strategy (big choice) has a validity date of 5 to 7 years.

24 **By diluting (1).** The dilution process also impacts the number of small options available for any given decision. Here's how the extra service might impact a call center manager: "We don't offer much service to 90 percent of our clients, but recently our company started offering more service to a few clients. Do I need to organize the call center in such a way that we can provide the extra service?" *(If the answer is yes, from that moment on, the call center needs to consider the impact of every decision on the service level of these new clients).* Here's how the dilution on the client side might impact the small choices for the product designer: "Our product features are set up for small clients. If we want to keep our two new big clients, do we need to add the kind of typical features that a big company expects?"

By diluting (2). Note that it's important to carefully manage the timeframe so as to not dilute the choice again. Don't say, "We're going to accept clients outside of our core activity until our financial situation is stable," but rather "We accept clients outside of our core segment when our backlog becomes shorter than 12 weeks," a clear measureable indicator. *We say 'yes' only when we get into short-term financial trouble.*

28 **Railway story.** The information is compiled from several sources including Brendan Martin (2002), "Railway privatization through concessions, the origins and effects of the experience in Latin America," "ERM the promise of private equity case studies from emerging markets," and "America Latina Logistica," Harvard Business School case (2004).

CHAPTER 3

34 **Gladwell's bestseller.** Malcolm Gladwell, *The Tipping Point*, Hachette Book Group. You find the quote about the Rule of 150 on p182.

35 **Sherlock Holmes.** Easy access to loads of interesting links via the Sherlock Holmes Wikipedia page, http://en.wikipedia.org/wiki/Sherlock_Holmes.

36 **Gordon Allport and Joseph Postman.** Gordon W. Allport and Léo Postman (1947), *The Psychology of Rumor.*

37 **String of commands.** The Hamlet example is found in several documents. My information came from Bauke Visser (1998), "Binary Decision Structures and the Required Detail of Information."

41 **Nico Croes.** Quote came from a discussion with the author.

43 **Distortion TV.** A few practical pointers:
(1) Make sure you get a good mix of people—the CEO, a few members of the management team, people from staff, and business lines.

(2) The answers themselves shouldn't run to more than a minute, but you will need 15 minutes to explain what you do to reassure

participants.

(3) If you are dealing with various global locations, you can instruct people to interview a few people at key locations and edit the material into one video.

(4) Ask people to speak in their native language and use subtitles. If edited with care, the effect can be quite powerful.

(5) Consider combining the video with a short survey to get the 'engineers' on board. The survey doesn't measure the strategy distortion but gives you a clear view on the quality of the strategy communication. And there is a strong correlation between the perceived quality of strategy communication and the amount of Strategy Graffiti you will find—the message deviation. Keep it simple. The goal is to have supporting material for the video, not to design a complete survey.

(6) Organize the debrief carefully. I suggest a 90-minute meeting with the senior management team or business unit using an existing platform. This could be an off-site, regular team meeting or event. The first part—lasting about 10 minutes—is used to show the Strategy Graffiti video and the next part to discuss the results. I have learned that it's best not to reveal too much upfront, but to show the video. This increases the emotional impact. This also provokes discussion as most people were unaware of the size of the issue before and need time to manage their surprise: *"I never thought it was so bad"*, their disbelief: "Are you sure this sample is from our company?", and their frustration: "We have worked so hard to communicate. How is this possible?" As a rule of thumb, don't run the video it you haven't got at least 45 minutes to discuss it afterwards. Once the team has accepted the reality, you can move towards the solution and discuss the Strategy Graffiti clean-up.

(7) Why a video? The video might look very effective because we make people feel the distortion. Let them feel the distortion. Don't tell them. (A rational explanation is not the best approach.

I will refer back to this point at a later stage). Let them feel the difference with the original visible.

CHAPTER 4

46 **In 1990.** Edwin Locke and Gary Latham (1990), *A Theory of Goal-setting & Task Performance*. They also published an interesting short paper 25 years after their ground-breaking research called "New Directions in Goal-setting Theory" (2006), Association for Psychological Science, Volume 15, No 5, pp265-268.

47 **Jef Schrauwen story.** Information based on discussions with the author.

49 **NASA.** Chris McChesney, Sean Covey and Jim Huling (2012), *The 4 Disciplines of Execution*, Simon & Schuster, UK. You can find the NASA quote on p39.

50 **NASA finish line.** Richard Rumelt (2011), *Good Strategy, Bad Strategy*, Profile Books Ltd. The quotes can be found on pp107-108.

47 **A finish line.** When I became a professional speaker a few years ago, I also needed a finish line. I came up with the following: "To speak to 50,000 people in 50 countries before I turn 50." Now, at the age of 40, I'm at 21,500 and 30 countries. You can find the list of countries on my blog www.jeroen-de-flander.com. If you think you can help me reach my finish line by organizing a session in a country that's not on this list, drop me an email.

CHAPTER 5

53 **The marathon.** The information can be found on the Athens marathon website, www.athensmarathon.com.

54 **Tomás Valcke.** Interview with the author.

55 **Body balance.** According to Valcke, each kg you lose accounts for a 3 to 4-minute time improvement at the finish line.

55 **Bart Yasso**. Check out Bart Yasso's website www.bartyasso.com for more information.

57 **Billy Beane.** This incredible story was the focus of the book *Moneyball: The Art of Winning an Unfair Game* (2003) by Michael Lewis on which the 2011 film *Moneyball* with Brad Pitt was based.

59 **Dr Hallowell and John Ratey.** Article in the *New York Times* by Matt Richtel (July 6 2003), "The Lure of Data: Is It Addictive?"

60 **Scoreboard quote.** Chris McChesney, Sean Covey and Jim Huling (2012), *The 4 Disciplines of Execution*, Simon & Schuster UK, p67.

53 **Signposts (1).** It's important to make the lead indicator information readily available. There's no point in having signposts if those traveling don't see them.

Signposts (2). Measurement is part of our DNA. As Andrew Robinson points out in *The Story of Measurement*, measurement has defined society, government, and progress since the dawn of civilization. Length, area, volume, angle, weight, value, language, and time all had to be quantified and systematized to mark out land, plant crops, build palaces, trade goods, tax individuals, keep records, and celebrate festivals. In science, measurement has given rise to the modern world with its cash registers, communication satellites, and brain scanners. It regulates almost every aspect of our lives—through exams, interest rates, drug prescriptions, and opinion surveys—whether we like it or not.

Signposts (3). Knowing that we're all biased when it comes to judging indicator importance, it's smart to involve others. They will give us the perspective we need to end up with the right measurement set. Our measurement challengers will also help you avoid a black and white approach. Once there's the *aha-er-lebnis* on measurement, there's a risk to start a 'kill all measures' crusade. And while doing this, lots of useless measures will disappear (which is great), but there's also a risk crucial indicators that you're unaware of in other departments, units or teams also end up on our wipe-out list.

Signposts (4). For the measures you decide to keep, it's important to *challenge the data collection process*. Stop asking players to provide data for the coaching dashboard. Team members can and should be responsibilized to collect information to track their own lead measures, but filling the coach's scoreboard is a job for the coach. So don't bother team players with this. A soccer coach doesn't ask his player to count the number of successful passes they make during a game and a tennis coach doesn't ask her player to count the number of forehand winning strokes. And Billy Beane didn't ask his players to count their runs either. Players have more important things to do than to collect data for someone else. They have a game to win.

Signposts (5). You may end up with a set of indicators that didn't get a positive response, but fall into a special category because you are 'forced' to track them. There is no value for you or your team, but someone higher up the hierarchy—the club manager—may need the information to make a decision. You won't be able to throw these measures in the trash, so your best course of action is to challenge firmly, but politely, the need to track these measures. And while you won't be able to cut out all the measures (not everyone is willing to stop their dopamine hit), every indicator is one less that puts you on the wrong track.

CHAPTER 6

66 **The Kidney Heist.** This urban myth can be found in Chip and Dan Heath (2008), *Made to Stick,* Arrow Books, p3.

66 **Psychologist Jerome Bruner.** Paul Smith (2012), *Lead with a Story,* American Management Association.

70 **The Zambia story.** Stephen Denning (2001), *The Springboard.* His quotes can be found on pp9, 10, 24 and 27. He also wrote *The Leader's Guide to Storytelling* that digs deeper into the storytelling topic.

68 **Knowledge management remains.** For more information about the priorities of the World Bank and the role of knowledge sharing today, have a look at their website http://www.worldbank. org. You can also download a very interesting 74-page document, "The state of World Bank knowledge services: knowledge for development," 2011.

71 **David Hurchens.** Mary Wacker and Lori Silverman (2003), *Stories Trainers Tell: 55 Ready-to-Use Stories to Make Training Stick,* Jossey-Bass Pfeiffer.

77 **An interesting study.** John P. Kotter and Dan S. Cohen (2002), *The Heart of Change,* Harvard Business Review Press.

73 **Josie King.** http://www.josieking.org/whathappened. With the help of others, both parents created the Josie King Foundation. Its mission is to prevent others from dying or being harmed by medical errors. "By uniting healthcare providers and consumers, and funding innovative safety programs, we hope to create a culture of patient safety, together."

72 **Donald Berwick.** The IHI keeps using stories to pass along key ideas. All participating hospitals are encouraged to share their success stories. On the IHI website (http://www.ihi.org/Pages/default.aspx), you can find 388 'improvement stories' (as they call them). They range from ideas to save lives in New Zealand to suggestions to improve internal communication processes.

74 **Aboriginals.** More info and links about Aboriginal storytelling can be found here: http://www.lib.sk.ca/Storytelling.

74 **Sto:lo community.** Jo-Ann Archibald (2008). *Indigenous Story-*

work: Educating the Heart, Mind, Body, and Spirit. Vancouver, British Columbia: The University of British Columbia Press.

74 **Marketers.** Seth Godin (2005), *All Marketers Tell Stories*, Portfolio Hardcover.

67 **Strategy stories.** The more a story resembles the context of the traveler, the more effective it will be. It might need to have several wrappings for the same idea.

76 **Jared Fogle's story.** I compiled Jared's story from several sources including Chip and Dan Heath (2008), *Made to Stick*, Arrow Books and the Subway website where you can learn more about Jared's 15-year journey, http://www.subway.com/subwayroot/freshbuzz/website/jareds_journey/.

CHAPTER 7

87 **Rhode Island Hospital story.** See Charles Duhigg (2012), *The Power of Habit*, Random House and Stephen Powell and Ruth Kimberly Hill, "My Co-pilot is a Nurse."

89 **Air Florida Airline Cockpit story.** I used several sources including Ute Fischer and Judith Orasanu, "Error Challenging Strategies: their Role in Preventing, Correcting Errors" and "Cultural Diversity and Crew Communication" and Malcolm Gladwell (2009), *Outliers*, Penguin.

92 **Crew Resource Management.** Rhona Flin, Paul O'Conor, and Margaret Crichton (2008), *Safety at the Sharp End, a Guide to Non-Technical Skills*, Ashgate.

93 **Serious cost savings.** One hospital, for example, reported savings of 2 million dollars a year.

94 **Newborn baby story.** Gary Klein (1998), *Sources of Power: How People Make Decisions*, MIT Press.

CHAPTER 8

97 **Roger Bannister**. Roger Bannister (2004 revised and enlarged edition), *The First Four Minutes*, Sutton Publishing.

98 **4-minute mile**. Since Roger Banister's magic race, thousands of people have run the mile in under 4 minutes. In the next 30 years, the world record was broken 15+ times. It now stands at 3 minutes and 43 seconds. The current record holder is Hicham El Guerrouj from Morocco with a time of 3:43.13. Even high school students have broken the 4-minute mile. In 1997, Daniel Komen of Kenya doubled the feat running 2 miles in less than 8 minutes.

99 **Albert Bandura.** I drew from several sources including Albert Bandura (1986) landmark book in psychology, *Social Foundations of Thought and Action: A Social Cognitive Theory* and (1998) "Organisational Applications of Social Cognitive Theory", Australian Journal of Management, 13.2., p275-302. Meta-analyses by Sadri and Robertson (1993), as well as Stajkovic and Luthans' (1998) wide-ranging methodological and analytic work-related laboratory and field studies provide overwhelming evidence that efficacy beliefs influence the level of motivation and performance.

103 **The Pygmalion Effect.** This was first discovered, proved, and coined by Professor Robert Rosenthal and Lenore Jacobson in 1968 using a classroom experiment. The effect was named after a play by George Bernard Shaw.

103 **Army experiment.** Dov Eden (1992), "Leadership and Expectations: Pygmalion Effects and Other Self-fulfilling Prophecies in Organizations," Leadership Quarterly, 3(4), pp271-305.

103 **Factory workers.** Dov Eden (1992), "Leadership and Expectations: Pygmalion Effects and Other Self-fulfilling Prophecies in Organizations," Leadership Quarterly, 3(4), pp271-305.

CHAPTER 9

113 **CO₂mplexity (1).** Let's be clear. Not all complexity is bad. External complexity gives companies the opportunity to create niches
and helps to avoid commoditization. Consider a telecom company offering call credits using different brands, each appeal-
ing to different customer segments. It makes tariff plans way
complex. Take advantage of this complexity. Internal complexity doesn't offer the same benefits. It's a self-created state where
only the company is to blame. But this complexity shouldn't find
its way inside the company walls. Successful strategists know
that external complexity creates business opportunities, while
internal complexity slowly kills them.

CO₂mplexity (2). Our email behavior also adds to internal complexity. Two Bain consultants, Chris Brahm and Eric Garton
(2012), recently studied 2,300 managers at a global industrial
company with 14,000 employees. As a group, these individuals
sent and received more than 260,000 emails a month to each
other. On top of that, the typical manager devoted 8 hours each
week to meetings—for senior managers the figure was more
like 20 hours—and the volume was growing. During the average
meeting, about a quarter of attendees sent at least 2 emails every 30 minutes. (*You wonder when these managers get any work
done, right?*). The article is called, "Your company is connected—
but can it make and execute good decisions?"

CO₂mplexity (3). Without having done proper research, I believe
you can categorize companies on 4 levels along a maturity scale
to combat internal complexity: Level 1: The organization doesn't
care about simplicity. Complexity reduction is non-existent.
Everyone keeps adding stuff. In an attempt to deal with external complexity, companies create internal complexity; Level 2:
Some individuals launch simplification initiatives on an ad hoc
and individual basis; Level 3: The organization actively supports
complexity reduction endeavors; Level 4: Reducing the complexity footprint is the norm for individuals, teams, and the whole

organization. The art of simplicity is embedded in the HR and performance management processes of the organization.

115 **Leo Babauta.** His motivational website is called *Zen Habits* and can be found at www.zenhabits.com. He has a second blog on minimalism that can be found at www.mnmlist.com.

117 **The Rule of 150.** It's also known as 'Dunbar's number,' named after the British anthropologist Robin Dunbar.

117 **According to.** Chris Zook and James Allen (2012), *Repeatability*, Harvard Business Review Press.

115 **Growth.** Growth is not a strategy, it's not a big choice. Growth is a consequence of a big choice.

119 **Tata's story.** I compiled the story from several sources including *Business Standard*, September 29, 2009 and the Tata Nano website, www.tatanano.com. It's interesting to know that Ratan Tata won The *Economist's* Innovation Award for Business Process Innovation in 2009. "Innovative ideas are everywhere," said Mark Langley, executive vice president and COO of the Project Management Institute. "What we salute with the Business Process Award is rarer: the implementation, through effective projects and programs that translates ideas into lasting change. Tata Motors' Nano challenges the way automobiles have been made and marketed for a hundred years. The application of project management is testimony to Tata Group's record of refining its processes, from boardroom to manufacturing floor, and promises transformation of an industry facing a billion new customers over the next generation."

CHAPTER 10

116 **Porter's classic Five Forces framework.** As mentioned before, a great book to get up to speed on the strategy essentials is *Understanding Michael Porter* by Joan Magretta (2012), Harvard Business Review Press.

129 **More examples.** Charles Duhigg (2012), *The Power of Habit*, Random House.

129 **Two professors.** Jeremy Dean (2013), *Making Habits, Breaking Habits*, Oneworld Publications.

CHAPTER 11

133 **Dixie Dansercoer.** For details on Dansercoer's journey, I am indebted to Dixie Dansercoer for generously giving me his time. I also drew from several of his books including *Beyond the Challenge*, Dutch edition by Snoecks.

134 **The idea was:** Here's a rough sketch of the initial route Dansercoer and Deltour envisioned.

135 **He found.** Roland Huntford (1999, updated edition), *The Last Place on Earth*, Random House.

136 **Implementation Intentions.** I drew from several sources including Peter M. Gollwitzer (1999), "Implementation Intentions: Strong Effects of Simple Plans," American Psychologist, Vol 54, No 7, pp493-503. Inge Schweiger Gallo and Peter M. Gollwitzer (2007), "A look back at 15 years of progress," Psychothema, Marieke Adriaanse and others, "Breaking Habits with Implementation Intentions: a test of Underlying Processes." Chip and Dan Heath (2010), *Switch*, Random House and Charles Duhigg (2012),

The Power of Habit, Random House.

139 **Jerry Seinfeld.** Jeremy Dean (2013), *Making Habits, Breaking Habits*, Oneworld Publications.

---The future is shaped by the decisions we make today---

Index

Ideas

Acknowledgements

Writing a book is a bit of a journey as well. And I've come across many twists and turns in the road over the last year. Luckily, I could count on others to guide me to the finish line.

First of all, a big thank you to all the researchers in the field. Unknowingly, you have provided gold nuggets to support the reasoning in this book. A special thank you to the research team from *the performance factory* for the long hours and commitment to this massive research project. And ShiftIn Partners, our partner in the Middle East. Thanks for sharing insights and enthusiasm to this project.

Thanks also to Siân Hoskins, my word wizard. Always there when I needed you. Never missing a deadline. And Paul Niven for reviewing an early manuscript and providing valuable insights.

Jana Keppens, my art master. And Paul Verhoestraete for the endless hours of drawing to translate ideas into vivid illustrations.

Dixie Dansercoer – thanks for taking the time to share your amazing experiences. Our discussions gave me a glimpse of what it's like to undertake impossible adventures.

Karen, Lauren, and Jonas for enduring an individual who was physically present, but lived in his head for several months.

And last, but not least, you, my dear reader. Thanks for reading. I truly hope the ideas in this book help you get your ideas to the finish line.